Praise for *Bedpan Banter*

This book has a message for everyone, whether you are a cancer survivor, friend, or relative of someone going through a health crisis. At some point in our lives we all face our own health battles and sometimes need to help others with theirs. *Bedpan Banter* will help us meet those challenges with these inspiring, thought provoking, tender, and humorous stories.

—*Deb Rodahl, System Director, HealthEast Laboratory Services*

This book is a display of the special power laughter brings out in all of us. This read is a rollercoaster of emotion, always ending in humor, but never doubting the person's strength in their story. What better way to learn than through the sharing of stories. This piece of work is a celebration of people and their ability to laugh during difficult times—truly the human spirit!

—*Kelly Kirwin, Director, Grand Itasca Foundation*

Bedpan Banter is a survival guide to accepting life's challenges. The stories are humbling, inspiring, and hysterical! Brenda shares her journey and humor while teaching us that it's okay to talk and find humor in the scary things.

—*Krista Waller, Colon Cancer Awareness Advocate,*
Ohio Valley Colon and Rectal Surgeons

Bedpan Banter demonstrates through a kaleidoscope of inspirational and humorous health related stories that it is not the journey, but our interconnectedness on the way, that enriches life and gives each of us the opportunity to "pay it forward" in the most unlikely of circumstances.

—*Julie Powell, RN, BSN, CWOCN, Fairview Southdale Hospital*

I enjoyed these stories. At times you laugh, other stories make you feel the author's pain and share their tears. We are reminded that healing is not always just about the medicine.

—*Mindy Brandmeyer, CRA, Martha Siekman Cancer Center*

If doctors could prescribe a good laugh for their patients, we'd probably have some healthier folks out there (but I wonder what the co-pay would be?). Brenda's right when she says humor can be found in a hospital, you just have to listen for it. Fortunately, *Bedpan Banter* can fill in the silences. Take it to your next colonoscopy!

—*Carlea Bauman, President, C3: Colorectal Cancer Coalition*

Brenda Elsagher has done it again. She's packed a book with hope, humor, and inspiration. There's at least one tale in this book that you will relate to and probably several stories that will sound like your own medical memories. Be prepared to have your guard lowered, your spirit lifted, and your humor capacity enlarged after spending time with *Bedpan Banter*.

—*San Short, RN, BSN, CDE Upson Regional Medical Center*

This collection of experiences from patients, both young and old, and healthcare providers, both nurses and physicians is outstanding. I enjoyed the diversity of stories including the importance of prayer, God, humor, pet therapy, and patients helping roommates, in addition to healthcare provider insight. My favorite chapter was Bowels Gone Berserk, but knowing I am a WOCN, this should not be surprising. The stories about the benefits of having an ostomy and challenge of body image change when you have an ostomy were my favorites. Many of the stories discussed stressful experiences with either a humoristic twist or in a manner that personal growth is identified. The positive hospital experiences cited is a tribute to the medical and nursing professions.

—*Kathleen Borchert, MS, RN, CWOCN, ACNS-BC, Bethesda Hospital*

Brenda Elsagher brings these stories to you with energy, spirit and an enduring sense of hope. She illustrates laughter, not as a tool to cope, but as a path to embracing life.

—*Scott Burton, author, entertainer and national keynote speaker*

Bedpan Banter

Medical Stories
of Humor and
Inspiration

Brenda Elsagher

BEDPAN BANTER © copyright 2009 by Brenda Elsagher
All rights reserved. No part of this book may be reproduced in any form whatsoever, by photography or xerography or by any other means, by broadcast or transmission, by translation into any kind of language, nor by recording electronically or otherwise, without permission in writing from the author, except by a reviewer, who may quote brief passages in critical articles or reviews.

ISBN 10: 1-931945-90-X
ISBN 13: 978-1-931945-90-5

Library of Congress Catalog Number: 2009927234
Printed in the United States of America

First Printing: May 2009

12 11 10 09 08   5 4 3 2 1

 Expert Publishing, Inc.
14314 Thrush Street NW,
Andover, MN 55304-3330
1-877-755-4966
www.ExpertPublishingInc.com

Dedication

To the first man I loved that knew how to tell a good story—Eugene John Elsen (Hump), my dad. As a child, I always looked forward to your returning from work. We as a family of ten would sit together and I felt happy, anxious to hear the stories of your day.

Even though we are both much older now, you still astound me with your ability to come up with more stories I have never heard. You taught me that *everybody* has a story.

And this book is dedicated to all the people who tell stories. Whether your stories are written or spoken, you know how healing a good story can be.

Table of Contents

Foreword

Jill Amundson Winter

The year was 1995, and by that time I had worked at various jobs in the same medical clinic for seven years. In my most recent job, as a referral secretary, I had both the misfortune and good fortune of seeing people at a time in their lives when they were most vulnerable—when they needed help. The patients came to my desk when they were told they needed to see a specialist or needed some testing done; these were usually the really sick patients or those who needed further urgent care.

While every patient mattered, certain patients stood out—made an impression. That's what happened when Brenda walked up to my desk. Her surgeon accompanied her to my desk; this was unusual. While he was a fine surgeon, he didn't exactly have a sparkling personality. Frankly, he was a grump, but his gruff exterior often hid what I knew was a deep concern for his patients. When he escorted a patient to my referral desk, I knew it was serious. I wondered what it would be as I watched the doctor and a youngish couple walking toward my desk. The couple was laughing and joking together while the doctor admonished me to schedule several tests and appointments for Brenda as soon as possible. As I reviewed the referral requests, Brenda's story started to unfold.

Brenda had come to the clinic to see her primary care physician one day because she thought she was suffering from hemorrhoids. While hemorrhoids are uncomfortable and embarrassing, they certainly aren't usually considered to be life threatening, and I imagine Brenda wasn't all that concerned about her appointment. However, her primary physician had her see the general surgeon who was working that day. She left the surgeon's office with a diagnosis of probable rectal cancer and then awaited the biopsy results.

When she came to my desk, three days had passed since she had been told she likely had cancer. Her biopsy results had come back, and her cancer diagnosis had been confirmed. She and her husband had just been told that she would need extensive surgery to remove the cancer, including a permanent colostomy, a hysterectomy, and would likely need vaginal reconstruction along with all the rest of it. At that point they had been married only six years and had two children ages five and three.

Brenda was razzing her husband mercilessly about how their sex life was going to change. With a wicked sparkle in her eye I heard her say, "Well, maybe you can put your order in for a custom fitted one..." I was truly amazed that they weren't both bawling their eyes out, and I marveled at what a truly special relationship Brenda and her husband must have had in order to laugh in the face of the possibility that their sex life could very well be altered in unimaginable ways with her diagnosis.

Brenda was back at my referral desk several times over the next many months to schedule various and sundry tests and appointments. She was always laughing and joking about her latest experiences, left a good impression, and the sparkle never left her eyes.

As if this story weren't improbable enough, another thing happened. The austere surgeon that performed her surgery was a changed man after treating Brenda. He had been completely unapproachable and was prone to yelling at clerical staff and nurses. He was angry all of the time. I think most other doctors were even afraid of him. Suddenly, it was like he had "found religion." He was friendly, kind, and personable, and I soon discovered that the only time now that he was crabby was when he had just seen a patient that he wasn't able to help. He hated not being able to help his patients, and he also became a real advocate for his patients. One of his campaigns was to make sure that breast reconstruction after mastectomy was covered by health insurance by law; he was ahead of his time in fighting for this to be resolved. He would stop at my desk and talk to me about this issue and even ask my opinion about it. I thought it was pretty unusual for an older male doctor, a Navy man at that, to even care about this, but he did—passionately, and I gained a whole new respect for him.

I really knew that the good doctor had seriously changed when he was at my desk one day and said, "Do you want to hear a joke?" Before meeting Brenda, I don't think he found anything funny.

Over the years, I followed Brenda's progress through the local media. She had decided to turn her rectal cancer into a comedy routine and had become quite successful. Who knew anyone could find something funny about rectal cancer? There were several articles written about her in the local papers, and I read every one of them like they were about a member of my family.

BEDPAN BANTER

Thirteen years after first meeting her, I was preparing to attend a conference, and noticed that Brenda was scheduled to be the keynote speaker. I was thrilled. I still worked for the same company, but in a more administrative role now, and I still felt a connection to her. As she spoke, telling about her cancer diagnosis and the years since, with her signature humor, it surprised me how personal and touching her story felt to *me*. My eyes welled up and I felt proud to be a part of her story, even if I was the only one who knew it. It made me realize that I was a part of her journey, and she was a part of mine. I can only hope that I helped clear some of the stones out of her path to make her journey a little easier, even as she taught me how to be grateful for what I have, rather than sorrowful for what I don't.

Brenda reminded me that my interactions with others, no matter how small, make a difference. Did Brenda know how many people she was touching as she skipped through that cancer mine field with unbridled joy? Probably not. But we were watching and learning from her, and I now have the blessed burden of trying to live an inspired life, just in case others are watching me.

Jill Amundson Winter
Credentialing Supervisor, HealthPartners

Acknowledgements

For my pals—Sherry Wenborg, Rox Tarrant, Jodie Maruska, Stephanie Maas, Renee Rongen, Monica Sausen, and Gail Fuad, who helped me sort through the many contributed stories, I appreciate the time you gave me. Thanks for the many occasions you allowed me to interrupt you so that we might talk through another story.

Thanks to Christine Dellwo, Kim, Laurie, and Amy Elsen for proofreading. Special thanks for helpful suggestions, Pat Dennis, Kris Versdahl.

Thanks to the many contributors for allowing me to include your rich stories in *Bedpan Banter*; it is an honor to share them. I appreciate your tolerance in editing your stories, and I look forward to reading your future work. Keep on writing and sharing your gifts.

To my friends at Hollister Incorporated, I am indebted to you for the opportunities you have provided for me to share my writing and speaking gifts. I appreciate and thank you for your trust and encouragement. Ladonna Cleveland, retired from Hollister Incorporated, will always have a special place in my heart.

To my friends Harry and Sharron Stockhausen at Expert Publishing who are always in my corner—many thanks.

To Mike Powless, OLM Designs for the cover design.

To Gil Martinez at Martinez Images for the great job in photography on the front and back covers.

Thanks to Kathy Fritz, RN, for being my cover model and my dear friend. And especially for my family John, Jehan, and Bahgat.

Introduction

I love the process of writing and the adventures that come along the way. The idea of writing a collection of medical stories of humor and inspiration came out of the work I have been doing as a speaker across the United States and Canada. Everywhere I went people wanted to tell me their funny stories and many of their stories were inspirational as well. Thus, began the idea for this, my third book, *Bedpan Banter*.

In April 2008, I was fortunate to attend the Erma Bombeck's humor writer's conference in Dayton, Ohio. I used that opportunity to connect with many skilled writers who later became contributors in this book. This was my second Erma Bombeck humor writer's conference. At the first one I attended, two years prior, I had the privilege to meet columnist and author Dave Barry. He mentioned he finds the humor in all things around us and he writes about everyday things we can all relate to, much like the late Erma Bombeck. He is a funny and prolific writer and told the crowd of writers attending that he didn't believe in writer's block. He said that every day he set out to write at least one thousand words, hoping most of them would be useful in the story. In just over a month, he could have a book written.

I know there is truth in sitting in your chair and getting the task done—my tush feels it right now. I can find so many things to distract me—email, the phone, or cleaning out that junk drawer I've been meaning to do since my daughter was in first grade. Uhhh, she's a junior in high school now. Last year, Garrison Keillor was the main speaker at the Erma Bombeck conference and he was very entertaining and practical with his writing tips. He said you had to get outside to write well. You had to go for walks, see nature and people, and get away from the computer. *Do long lunches with friends count?* I wondered. He was empathetic with us writers, and at the same time, encouraging and inspiring. I had heard he was unapproachable and sullen. Instead, he came across interested and full of compassion.

I didn't choose to stand in the long line to meet Keillor because I needed to get away from people. Sometimes I am like that, so up to my room I went and played with the remote, madly watching five shows at a time. Since we have only the basic network broadcast channels at home, this was still a treat. It's the little things that make me happy.

INTRODUCTION

I must admit even though the conference was ripe for networking, that thought didn't occur to me until it was half over. From then on, every time there were more than twenty-five people gathered in a room, I made the announcement about *Bedpan Banter* and that I needed great medical stories sent to me. I would quickly pass out my business cards before the next speaker would start and then I would repeat the process all over again at lunch, dinner, or on the bus with the writers back to the hotel. It was fun to see how my pleas helped strangers talk with each other.

I received many stories from those conference announcements. Other stories came from friends, family members, health care professionals, and all sorts of writers across North America. It was hard to turn away stories, but I wanted to stay with the funny or inspiring theme throughout the book. The contributors were most gracious if their story required a little editing, and it was a pleasure to work with each of them. I hope to meet every one of them someday.

It seems like medical stories are something most people can relate to, and as I age, I noticed medical topics and trips to the hospital sometimes compete with discussions about music, movies, politics, or even our children. Being in the hospital is the great leveler. When you are walking around in your hospital gown, your hair in a cap and those little booties on, no one knows if you are the president of a bank or a singing waiter—unless, of course, you burst out in song as they wheel you out of surgery.

Stories can be healing as we learn to cope with a health challenge either we or a loved one is facing. A long time ago I chose to look for the humor in the situations I found myself in at the clinic or hospital. Just watch, humor is all around you. One time on my way to the surgical floor to await surgery, I heard the nurse call down the hall, "Are your privates clean?" I started laughing and then she realized how that sounded as she inquired about the condition of the room.

My path took a turn as I faced cancer and the physical challenges that came with it. I began to speak publicly about having had colon cancer, and was challenged. The subject was still far from being a mainstream message, and I lacked experience about speaking in public. Then someone gave me some good advice—be yourself, tell your stories, and it will work out. I still worried about giving talks to health professionals and not having the academic credentials they might like. One day I was lamenting about it to my friend Renee. "I think they would prefer I have credentials after my name, and I am nowhere close to having them," I commented. "Make some up," my wise friend said. Then we laughed about the wild prospects I suggested.

Just for fun one day when I was about to talk to a group of nurses, I decided to include LRF after my name on the PowerPoint presentation. It remained on there for at least ten presentations until one nurse asked, "Brenda, I noticed you have credentials after your name that I don't recognize. What does LRF mean?" I told her, "I was intimidated to speak before such a knowledgeable crowd such as you. I thought I should have some fancy credentials too, so I made them up. They mean, Living Rectum Free." Everyone laughed and my credentials have been there ever since.

There are times when there is nothing funny about a medical crisis and we are grateful that the doctors and nurses work so diligently to make us well. And, as they say in the comedy world, time plus tragedy can bring on some good laughs. There are many stories in this book that probably didn't start out too funny either. Not too long ago, I was having major back spasms and the pain was unbearable. It radiated from my back across my hip, down my thigh, through the knee, and stayed as a major cramp through the front of my leg for hours. I awaited a phone call from the nurse with suggestions on what to do. Soon the phone rang and I looked at the name on the phone through blurred, tear-filled eyes. "Hello?"

"Brenda, this is Marilee, I'd like to go over a couple of things with you."

I went into a litany of my back symptoms, chiropractic care, history of problems, and concerns of needing something for the pain as well as muscle relaxants or something to get me through the weekend while I had to travel. I talked about a tragedy with a friend. "At least I'm not crying right now; it's been a bad day," I said as I sniffled.

"It sounds like it's been a bad day for you. I wanted to go over a few things in regard to your performance at the art center for the October event," she said.

With horror, I realized I had just blabbed all my weaknesses and sad day to a client, *not* the nurse at my clinic.

INTRODUCTION

When I said, "This is Marilee? From the upcoming comedy event in October? You are not my nurse!" I burst out laughing when I thought about what that poor woman had to listen to for the previous few minutes. A blubbering woman who was having a very bad day. "Well, you just got to know a lot about me. I'm sorry." Then we both laughed some more.

"I thought it was great you felt that comfortable to tell me all that," she offered.

"That's the first laugh I've had all day, thanks." Then we went on to talk business. It turned my day around to have laughed that hard and I felt better. Just two hours later all my spasms stopped and I could stand up straight and bend over and pick up things off the floor for the first time in three days. I am convinced laughter heals.

Hardly anyone escapes getting to middle age or old age without medical intervention of some kind. We can't take ourselves too seriously. If you can't laugh at yourself, then you are in real danger of suffering some major damage. My husband's best friend, Sherif, loves to laugh. He's the kind of guy who creates a party when he walks in the door, even if there are only two people, including him. This jovial man has not escaped his share of health challenges in the past, yet he frequently says, "Life is good; life is beautiful." He always wants us to enjoy the day—the moment. It's a simple, good philosophy. Life is good when I am writing and it's a beautiful life to share these stories with you. I hope you enjoy *Bedpan Banter* as much as I enjoyed bringing it to you.

—Brenda Elsagher

Hospital Happenings
Brenda Elsagher

The first doctor I fell in love with was the dashing Dr. Joe Gannon (Chad Everett) of Medical Center. I got all tingly when he came on the screen with those penetrating eyes of his. Marcus Welby, M.D. (Robert Young) was very talented, but he was no Chad. He did have his sidekick, Dr. Steven Kiley (James Brolin), who was cute and the coolest motorcycle driving doctor around. But the intensity of Chad's concern for the patient as the music swelled for the life threatening decision he'd have to make each week always got to me.

I didn't get into any television medical shows after that until *Chicago Hope, ER,* and *House*. Were there any? Who can forget puppy-eyed Dr. Doug Ross (George Clooney), the pediatrician who could fix the most amazing problems that arose week after week.

As I write this, we have the McDreamy doctor on *Grey's Anatomy* and all the doctors and nurses are very good looking but emotionally constipated. I don't care, it's still good entertainment. Supposedly the show is designed after real life hospital scenes. You might see a doctor pulling a hatchet out of the patient's head and the patient still survives. There usually is some cutting edge surgery that only one person seems to know, a visiting doctor who happens to be there for the right patient at the exact necessary time. I love it when things work out like that.

I asked my ten nurse girlfriends if they work in any kind of environment similar to these shows and no was their unified answer, but there was the occasional Dr. McDreamy. Still, no one comes close to my Chad. While the stories in this section may not be dramatic enough for a television series, they come from real people in real situations and that qualifies them enough to make you glad to read them.

Music Speaks Volumes
Cappy Hall Rearick

I squirmed on the cracked, fake-leather recliner in search of a comfortable position. It was Christmas Eve and cold outside, but stifling hot in the hospital room. As miserable as I was in the recliner, that was not the case with my mother. She was in the bed next to my chair in a coma, feeling nothing, I hoped, but a well-earned sense of peace.

I gazed out the window at the strings of red and green lights blinking on and off. It wasn't fair that Mama and I should spend this holy night in the hospital, but nobody ever said life was supposed to be fair, did they?

My mother stirred and I reached over to grasp her hand. I hoped she would open her eyes and say, "What's up, Doc?" or something silly. That was her former personality, always cracking jokes to ease the pain.

"Hey, Mama," I said softly. "It's me, Cappy. I don't know if you can hear me, but I want you to know I'm here. You're not alone." I'd read somewhere that it was important to say things like that to someone in a coma. "Talk to them," it said, "as though they are hearing every word."

As her only daughter, I'd flown to South Carolina as soon as Mama was diagnosed, knowing I might be there for several months, which I was. I bought books on how to deal with dying and how to say good-bye because I didn't know how to do either. I'd also packed healing oils that smelled like stale eucalyptus, relaxation tapes, and enough affirmations to restore my mother's health.

A no-nonsense woman, Mama would look at me with skeptical eyes when I spouted what she called my California WooWoo. "Visualize those cancer cells going down the drain when you take a shower, Mama." While I thought the analogy was just fine, she thought I was nuts.

So there I was on Christmas Eve, sitting quietly beside her bed wishing I didn't feel so helpless. The only sound in the room came from gurgling IV tubes attached to her.

Christmas music sure would be nice, I thought, and at that moment, the spark of an idea began to take shape.

My mother loved the Big Band sounds of her youth. Even on her seventieth birthday, Frank Sinatra still made her swoon, Sammy Kaye made her swing and sway, and Spike Jones made her laugh. At home, she played the albums over and over, especially while painting the delicate pieces of porcelain for which she had become known.

I squeezed her hand. "I'm going out, Mama. Don't go anywhere 'til I get back, okay?" I grabbed my coat and was out the door, thankful that the store where America shops never closes and that they stocked portable tape players.

After shopping, I drove to Mama's house for Frank Sinatra tapes, delighted to find one of his Christmas albums. Humming to myself, I returned, to her hospital room, with my arms loaded with music, happy to be doing at least something. It wouldn't cure her cancer, but I was confident that hearing the music she had loved all her life would get through to her.

"Mama, I'm back, and I brought Ol' Blue Eyes with me!"

Sinatra's distinctive sound soon filled the room. Glancing at Mama, I hoped for a smile of recognition, but her expression remained unchanged. On the other hand, when Ol' Blue Eyes sang "I'll Be Home for Christmas," I cried like a baby.

While the tape continued with holiday songs, I sniffled and watched more cars passing below, people going home to healthy loved ones. Hearing a soft knock on the door, I wiped away the fresh tears.

"May I come in?" It was a woman about Mama's age who looked even more tired than I felt. "I'm Helen from down the hall. The door was cracked and I heard music when I passed by. It sounded wonderful. May I hear some more?"

I grinned at the woman, happy for the company. "Do come in," I said. "I'm so glad you stopped by. I'm Cappy and this is my mom." I paused. "Do you like Sinatra?"

She smiled, and for a moment I saw the beautiful young woman she had once been. She was still lovely, and became even more so when Sinatra began to sing "Silver Bells." Her troubled face lost all the worry lines.

"Like him? I used to date him," she said.

Right, I thought. *Like I used to date JFK.*

She recognized my disbelief and laughed. "It was a million years ago, honey, but it's the truth. We dated for about six months." Her eyes twinkled. "You weren't even born then."

Suddenly captivated, I ditched my cynicism in order to hear more, and I didn't care if her story was a fantasy.

Plopping down on the battered old chair, I put my elbows on my knees and cupped my chin in both hands.

"What was Frank Sinatra really like?"

"Skinny," she said. "Skinniest man I ever saw, and such big feet. I bet he wore a size twelve shoe. He was a snazzy dresser, though. A regular clothes horse."

Big feet was not how I pictured the man, and for a moment I was afraid that Helen's description might burst Mama's long-held Sinatra bubble. There was something earnest in the way she spoke.

"But was he nice? Sweet or unsweet?" I asked.

Before answering, she cocked her head to the side and gestured toward the tape deck.

"Just listen to that voice. He's singing my favorite Christmas song."

Reaching over, I turned up the volume. The words, "Jack Frost nipping at your nose" floated through the air.

We listened quietly together. She crossed and uncrossed her legs and then smoothed her dress to cover her knees.

"Yes, he was nice. He was on his way up, so he was nice when it counted. He knew I couldn't help him become the star he aimed to be, but I was pretty and I knew which fork to use."

She looked at me with her old eyes, faded from what I imagined had once been a startling color of green.

"I always knew I was only a spoke in his wheel of life and that's all I'd ever be. When he left me that winter without even saying good-bye, I wasn't surprised. It was fun while it lasted and that was the lesson I was supposed to learn. Now when I hear him sing, well, I just sit back and enjoy what was."

After jump-starting her memory with a few more Sinatra ballads, she stood.

"I thank you for making an old lady feel young again. I'll bet your mother felt the same way, too."

I hugged her. I really hugged her and it felt good.

As though anticipating my question, she said, "Yes, it was hard letting go of my feelings for Frankie, but then I met Edward. He knows about my fling and likes to tease me about my movie star boyfriend." She grinned. "We were married fifty-one years ago. He's been here for over three weeks now, but his doctor said today that he won't be coming home again."

She looked tired, sad, and suddenly very much her age. "I'm so sorry," I offered.

A wistful smile played across her lips.

"Don't be. I'd forgotten my lesson in letting go, but hearing Frankie tonight brought it all back. I needed a reminder more than ever."

We hugged again before she left. I never imagined that Mama's favorite music would reach another person and touch them so profoundly.

I looked over at Mama as I walked past her bed and when I did, I saw her eyes were open and focused directly on me. She wore the sweetest expression, such a decided difference from the pale, slack face to which I had become accustomed.

Rushing to her side, I broke down and sobbed. I tried to talk, but I was crying so hard I didn't make a lick of sense. Mama's eyes followed me and remained locked on mine, although she didn't attempt to speak. When Sinatra began to sing "Silent Night," I stopped crying, almost as though he had directed me to be quiet.

I held my mother's hand while we listened together to that quintessential song of Christmas. I held on until the last "sleep in heavenly peace" was sung. Then she closed her eyes and, shepherded by the memory of Sinatra singing "Silent Night" to her, very quietly Mama left this world for good.

Unlike Sinatra, however, who left Helen without even a simple fair-thee-well or howdy-do, my mother's eyes had opened just long enough to tell me good-bye.

I kissed her softly and then let go of her hand knowing that Mama would always have a hold on my heart.

Closed Exit

Bob and Vella Owens

In 1998, Bob returned to the hospital room following colon surgery that involved removing his rectum. With amusement, we read the sign posted above his bed, "Do not use rectal thermometer."

Over the years at his yearly checkup, the doctor always wants to do a prostate check. Without thinking, the doctor asked him to get off the table and grab his ankles.

Bob reminds him, "I have an ileostomy."

Still not paying attention, while putting on his gloves, the doctor answers, "Yeah."

Bob bends over.

The doctor says in a surprised voice, "You're sewed up!"

Bob smugly said, "Yeah, good luck with that!"

The Visitors

Joyce Richardson

It was to be my brother-in-law's final trip to the hospital. The Appalachian visiting nurse, who had just taught Phil and me how to give Bob insulin shots at home, now looked at her patient in horror.

"To the emergency room," she commanded, noting Bob's dehydration and general state of being. And that is where my husband and I took him.

We knew Bob was a train wreck. Only one-fourth of his heart was functioning, his kidneys were failing, he was diabetic, and neuropathy rendered his feet numb. We lived in southeastern Ohio in the foothills of the Appalachians, and the nearest heart hospital was in Columbus, seventy-five miles away. Bob had been there before, and after an examination in our small-town Athens hospital (where the man next to us in the ER had been stabbed by his wife), we were destined to go again.

Bob wanted Phil and me to drive him to Columbus, but the hospital physician did not fancy his dying en route, so we waved good-bye as he settled into his passive patient role. As the ambulance drove off to Columbus, I noted the time: twelve midnight.

The next morning Phil and I got on the road, after boarding Bob's dog, a fat opinionated beagle, at the local kennel. We decided to stay in a motel on the Ohio State University campus, one that gave significant discounts to the relatives of patients, because we had a feeling this time the prognosis was not good. But hell, we'd been through this so many times before, we believed the Three Musketeers, as we called ourselves, would pull through once again.

I even looked forward to seeing Bob in his new digs, an intensive care, step-down room, whatever that meant. Bob, a former journalism professor and writer of a fishing column, had been all he-man. He was one of my favorite people. In earlier, more innocent times, I would take him cigarettes and cheeseburgers and thick chocolate milkshakes whenever he was incarcerated. But that was before he was diagnosed as diabetic and before cigarettes became taboo. Now he watched his diet carefully, but succumbed to cigarette-like cigars, which he claimed he never inhaled. Still, I spoiled him on each visit to the hospital and told him I would get him anything he wanted. He usually wanted a babe and his flirtations with nurses were legend.

His nurse, thinking I was serious about adding fat and sweets to his diet, told me to check with her later in the day and maybe she and I could work something out. Bob had no appetite at all. He complained about the food as he picked and picked. I cut up his meat and hand-fed him while he entertained us with stories about his night at the hospital after the ambulance squad had wheeled him in.

First he told us about a doctor coming to visit him—it must have been about four o'clock in the morning. Bob had asked the doctor about the wisdom of drinking alcohol in his condition. The doctor told him that four ounces a day would be fine, no more, no less. So, Bob said, looking at me out the corners of his eyes, "I think, maybe a martini."

Thinking that Bob was pulling my leg, I agreed with a smile. Then I said, "You produce the doctor and I'll produce the martini." I knew that no doctor in his right mind would say this, with Bob's various medications and his past record of abuse. Bob's reaction told me that he truly believed in the doctor, whether I did or not.

Then he told us that at night, the paintings in the room changed colors. Bob was an artist, so this seemed more logical than his other story. "What kind of paint did the artist use to change colors that way?" he asked one of his nurses. "It really is amazing!"

This nurse said he didn't know, and I examined the paintings with new interest.

"You know, I think the changing colors might be in your imagination," I told him, not wanting to lose him to another world.

"But they do," he said. "Stay this evening and see for yourself. And you won't believe who came to visit me last night," Bob said a few minutes later.

Like a couple of trained owls, Phil and I both asked, "Who?"

"Right where you're sitting, next to the drapes, I saw an elderly woman and a man who looked like Ernest Hemingway. I didn't even see them come in. But they smiled at me as if they knew me."

All I could say was, "Oh, my!" Phil didn't say anything. Neither of us looked at the other.

Bob seemed to be searching my face before he spoke. "Now them, I'm not sure about because their forms just kept fading into the curtains and finally they were gone."

"Ghosts," I said, although I didn't believe I had a spiritual bone in my body.

"But why?" he asked.

"Let me think about it," I answered.

When our visiting day was over, the nurse told us, "Hold off on the cheeseburger and milkshake delivery. Bob is going to have more blood tests this evening; I don't want his blood sugar screwed up. Maybe tomorrow, we'll talk about it."

There almost wasn't a tomorrow. When we visited Bob the next day we found out that early in the morning his heart had gone into an irregular rhythm. All day Bob introduced us to the members of his "pit crew," the doctors and nurses who had worked over him for over an hour. Bob had been a sports and racing car enthusiast, so the term pit crew conjured up a Bob kind of picture.

"If I'd gotten you a cheeseburger, I'd have blamed myself for your heart going out of kilter," I mused.

"You'd have jumped out the window, just like Ernest and the old woman," Bob said.

"Your visitors came back?" By this time I had a theory on these transparent people, but I didn't want to tell anyone, Bob especially. Nor had I said anything to Phil.

"They jumped?"

"Not really. Like the first night, they sat in front of the window, but neither came or went in any ordinary way."

I nodded my head.

The day progressed with tests and more tests and the nurses bringing Bob extra juice and a thick turkey sandwich with cheese. Bob joked with everyone. It was a good day.

"Spirit guides," I said to my husband that evening as we walked outside the motel. We had eaten well, buoyed up by Bob's cheerfulness and the fact that their sister was coming to Columbus to visit Bob the next day.

"Spirit guides?" Phil looked at me as if I were crazy.

My mother's relatives were spiritualists in the days of mediums and séances. Many times I heard Mom tell stories of séances where each participant was assigned a spirit guide who would take them into the next world.

"Ernest Hemingway," I said. "Not just someone who looked like him, but the man himself, will take Bob across the river and into the trees."

"And the old woman?"

"Bonnie, maybe?" I said, referring to their older sister who had died two years earlier.

"Except they didn't take him," Phil said. "The nurses and doctors saved his life."

"But they're waiting." I shivered in the cool May evening.

The phone call came early the next morning. Bob's heart had failed again. The pit crew did their best but had not succeeded this time. Around his bed I was certain the paintings on the walls gleamed in brilliant colors, as two figures guided Bob, martini in hand, to a place we can only imagine.

Limited Exposure
Kathy Fritz

I was working at North Memorial Hospital in Minnesota after I graduated; I worked in the Medical Surgery Department. There was an elderly confused gentleman, who was always exposing himself, especially to the young students. One of the students told Mrs. Erickson, an older nurse who had worked at North for a number of years. She had experience with this patient and said that she would handle the situation.

She walked into the patient's room, and said to the gentleman, "Okay, show me what you've got." He proceeded to show her and her reaction was to start laughing hysterically.

"I've seen bigger on a monkey!" she said and walked out of the room. There were no further problems with that patient.

The Undercover Cat Caper
Lois Fink

Muffin sensed something was wrong when Dad didn't come home. Where once they spent many afternoons together—Dad snoring softly while Muffin napped and purred—the recliner sat empty. Muffin circled the chair several times daily, stridently meowing her displeasure at Dad's absence. If Mom sat in the recliner, Muffin stoically refused her offers of companionship. Not only was Muffin disconcerted by Dad's disappearance, Dad was also missing Muffin's affection. Pet therapy was years away, but in 1994, I took matters into my own hands, and convinced the oncologist to authorize a pet visit; permission from hospital security came several days later.

A bath would be required for Muffin before her upcoming hospital visit. Though she was declawed, she still climbed trees, sashayed about the condominium complex, looked for insects to bait, bit the tails off lizards, and chased baby squirrels, her long, white fur turning a light brown as she crawled through the Phoenix vegetation staking out her territory. Unlike most cats, Muffin loved water, so coaxing her into the tub wasn't difficult and soon, with the aid of my nephew Howie, we lathered her with shampoo. Her insistent purring while relaxing under the gentle massage, rinsing, towel drying, and being brushed with a hair dryer told us she was enjoying the attention.

An hour later we rolled the fluffed, cleaned, and coiffed cat into a large blanket, and piled into the car for the short ride to the hospital. We walked into the hospital carrying Muffin as if she were a baby. Pressing the elevator button for the oncology unit, we crowded in with other visitors and the ascent seemed to take forever. To my horror, I noticed Muffin's tail had slipped through the blanket, twitching rapidly back and forth. Trying to be discreet, I nudged my nephew and said in a low voice, "The tail, the tail. Get it back in the blanket." No sooner had I uttered those words, when Muffin began meowing! Shifting Muffin in his arms, Howie swiftly scooped her tail back into a fold in the blanket. An elderly woman standing next to him commented on our unusual baby.

"She's unique," I muttered, as the door finally opened to our floor. We raced out of the elevator, conscious of the eyes following us. We stood catching our collective breaths, thankful there were no nurses or physicians nearby. Howie readjusted the blanket around Muffin's head so only her eyes were visible and we headed down the corridor to Dad's room.

We walked into the room and stood at the foot of Dad's bed.

"Dad, we have a surprise for you," I said.

Once she saw Dad, Muffin could no longer be contained. She leapt out of the blanket, landing next to him. He rested his hand on Muffin's back and she settled down, purring loudly. Muffin remained by Dad's side during the entire visit, never moving, as he continued stroking her back. My father's face, which up until then had been etched with pain and fear, was now relaxed. There was a sense of peace and acceptance that my mother, Howie, and I could not only see, but feel.

That was the only trip that Muffin took to the hospital; it was their final good-bye. I will never forget the look on my Dad's face as he gazed at Muffin and at us—it was filled with gratitude and love.

Girly-Girl
David Ayres

You would have to know my wife; her lady friends call her a "girly-girl." To me she is feminine and likes to look nice all the time. I had been married to this wonderful woman for nearly twenty-two years when we found out that she had stage 3 colorectal cancer. Surgery followed soon after radiation and chemo treatments. She reluctantly listened to the pre-surgery rules that said the hospital gown must be worn and no make-up or painted nails allowed.

While the surgery and temporary ileostomy took nearly four hours, I nervously paced the hospital hallways. My wife had been in recovery for thirty minutes by the time the surgeon came out to see me. The surgeon commented that she looked unusually well for going through a pretty tough surgery. *Kind words,* I thought as I expected to see a pasty white, groggy woman. This was not the case; I could not believe how well she looked; her color was terrific and this was only a half an hour after surgery.

How could anyone look this good? I thought.

A few days passed and my wife leaked out her secret that she had applied self tanner before surgery. "Hey, they said no make-up, but they didn't say no self tanner!" She said laughingly.

It did not take long for my wife and the surgeon to find some humor in teasing each other from the first meeting. And now that the surgery was over, she had a post op appointment with him. She wore a pretty red dress with matching red sandals. This was only two weeks after some major surgery. I was surprised that she had painted toe nails and could not figure out how she did this with abdominal stitches. She confessed later she painted her toenails before surgery because she knew she wouldn't be bending over for awhile.

As the surgeon watched her enter the room, he greeted her and said, "Your red dress and red shoes are pretty but the pink toenail polish does not match."

I thought to myself, *No, you didn't say that; you will pay.*

Without hesitation my wife responded, "Yeah, but your incision below my belly button is crooked. I am a Libra and things need to be balanced and straight," she continued. We all laughed.

Quite a woman I married, she's my girly-girl.

I'm Outta Here

Bob Simpson

In 1991, my wife was in the hospital sharing a room with a woman named Connie. The curtain was always drawn, so we never actually saw her. Connie was there for some tests for her heart, but it turned out to be a case of stress with no apparent heart problems. She had been the sole caregiver for her disabled husband for three years.

All the non-invasive tests had been done and results were normal. The last time we heard Connie behind the curtain was when her young cardiologist visited her on Tuesday night. He was suggesting a diagnostic heart catheterization in the morning and she had many questions.

"Has anyone ever died while you did the test?"

He said, "No."

"How many people die on average when this is done?"

He replied, "Only about one in a 1,000."

She asked him, "How many have you done?"

He replied, "Almost a thousand."

We never got to know Connie better; she checked herself out the next morning and went home.

Classical Gas

Diane Amadeo

If Charles Schultz was alive and Snoopy was typing a letter from atop his red doghouse, it would have started like this: Daybreak was dark and stormy...

We were in the midst of a triple digit heat wave. A cold front had moved in the wee morning hours causing a fierce thunderstorm. I know all this because of my sleepless visits to the porcelain bowl.

After running out of frivolous reasons to cancel the dreaded hospital test, the day of reckoning had arrived. I had done my preparations and secured transportation.

"We should be home by noon, no sweat," I had promised my adult daughter when asking for a ride. "If you have something planned, that's fine, I'll just cancel my appointment."

Just my luck, she had no plans until 2:00 p.m. Then she was going sailing with friends. On this appointed day, it didn't look good for sailing. Despite the inclement weather and rush hour traffic, we got to the hospital very early.

"Okay, I'll just drop you off and pick you up at noon," said my daughter with a yawn.

"They want you to stay," I said sheepishly.

She groaned, found a parking place, and escorted me in.

Admission procedure completed, we found the waiting room two hours early. We chatted while watching the downpour and lightening outside. Suddenly, there was a crack of thunder and the lights went out. Black smoke began to billow from the air conditioning unit outside the window. Generator lights flashed on.

"That is a bad omen," my daughter said.

Just then, the nurse called my name.

"It's an hour early," I said with delight. "We should be out of here by eleven."

Despite my current benign status, I did admit on the admission form to having multiple sclerosis (MS). Nowhere, however, did I mention to being a registered nurse (RN). I had left nursing a decade ago when my MS became active and I was in a wheelchair. I was just recently enjoying a hopefully prolonged remission period. Medicine had changed a lot this past decade. I didn't want anyone to assume I knew anything, even if it was just for a routine colonoscopy.

So I listened, mostly mute, to the many instructions, watched the IV placement, and asked the anesthesiologist if I would be able to watch the procedure on a monitor.

"Do you really want to?" he asked.

"Not really," I answered. I just thought I should act interested. "Frankly, I'd rather watch one on the Discovery Channel."

He laughed. "See you in a half hour or so," he said, while pushing a sedative into the IV tubing.

I slowly awakened in the noisy recovery room, thinking, *my, that was quick*. I asked the nurse, "What time is it?"

"Just past noon," she said.

"Noon!" I suddenly panicked. My daughter would be worried or furious. I tried to sit up but was entangled in tubing. There was a gauze bandage over the previous IV site. The IV was now in my other hand. There were five bandages over other attempted sites.

"Can you pass gas?" The nurse asked.

"Huh? No. No desire. But I do need to urinate."

She helped me up to the bathroom. I couldn't go.

"Neurogenic bladder," I explained. "MS, I'm just tickled my legs work."

My abdomen was becoming distended with gas. My bladder felt like it was going to burst.

"Can you get my daughter? She must be worried."

"You really want your daughter here?" another nurse asked.

In my grogginess, I attempted to explain how helpful my daughter has been during my crisis with the MS struggles, and how she was a tremendous support.

"You are lucky," the first nurse said and I agreed.

My daughter arrived, looking far from worried. She was laughing.

"You can't pee or fart? Wow, Mom, that's a first. Normally you can't bend over without tooting."

It wasn't funny, but in my medicated state, it was absurdly hilarious. Soon she had me in stitches.

"Keep her laughing," a third nurse said. "Maybe she'll have an accident and get some relief."

I wanted to ask about my missing hours, but kept forgetting.

"What did the doctor say?" my daughter asked.

Nurse Two overheard and started to giggle.

"I don't know; he hasn't been here," I said.

"Oh, he was here," Nurse Two said with a laugh. "Everything's fine, all is normal."

I suddenly recalled the faint words from a man's voice,

"She started moving during the procedure and we found the IV infiltrated and had to start all over again…she had normal results."

"I won't need to repeat this test for another five years," I said.

"Ten," Nurse Three said with a grin. "The doctor distinctly said, 'I don't want to see her again for ten years.'"

Everyone started laughing. *What the hell did I do? Kick him in the family jewels?*

"Nurses are the worst patients," Nurse One chimed in.

Uh-oh. I must have gotten sassy.

Gas pains start. Bladder spasms continue. I have to void badly, but I find it all funny. I laugh between moans. *Why do I keep seeing psychedelic colors and Mason Williams on guitar playing "Classical Gas"?*

"What helps your neurogenic bladder?" asked Nurse One.

"Knee chest position," I say, "Good for flatulence, too." Assisted into the knee chest position, it occurs to me that my daughter is in the line of fire. She notices too and more laughs followed, but no relief. My legs grow numb, and I am assisted to the side of the bed. My daughter plops into the chair beside me. The many position changes have caused blood to back up in the IV tubing. My daughter watches intently as Nurse Two flushes saline into the line.

"Are you a nurse, too?" asked Nurse Two.

"No, I'm an elementary school teacher." She seems mesmerized by the IV, the saline flush. Her eyes don't leave the procedure.

Nurse One says, "Why don't you take your mom for a walk? That may get the gas and bladder moving."

My daughter stands, then weaves and as the color drains from her face, her lips turn blue. Nurse Three and Nurse Two leapt into action.

"Sit down, put your head between your knees!" they commanded while they assisted her. Nurse One frowns as I began to laugh hysterically.

"She can't take the sight of blood, I presume," said Nurse Two, holding my daughter's weakened body in place on the chair.

"Guess not," I responded. "This is the reason why doctors didn't want husbands in the delivery room," I told my daughter between medicated laughs.

Nurse One seems slightly annoyed. I don't seem to be helping things.

"I'll take you on that walk," Nurse One said. I am holding my stomach in laughter, well aware this probably isn't amusing to the staff. My daughter is in good hands. It is four o'clock and the busy unit is empty, save for my daughter who now resides sheepishly in my bed with a cold compress on her forehead. The laughter, position changes, and walking have been conducive to much needed elimination relief.

"As soon as she is up and able to drive, I'm leaving," I inform the nurses.

"We hate to have you leave and perhaps return in agony," Nurse Two says, unconvincingly.

"I'll be okay," I say, much to their relief.

"I called Dad while you were walking; he was laughing so hard he could hardly talk."

I smirk, and think, *can't wait 'til it's his turn.*

"You get the car; I'll get dressed," I say while signing my name to multiple releases. *Gas pains cramp, my kingdom for a fart.*

In the car, we still laugh, "It's a beautiful sunshiny late afternoon. I'm sorry you missed your sail."

"No problem, the storm pushed back everything; they are picking me up at six," said my daughter.

I leaned back in the seat. My body relaxed and my kingdom comes. I can see Snoopy pull the paper from the typewriter, look out, and wiggle his eyebrows devilishly. His typed paper floats gently to the ground and reads, "Success comes from hard work and a few laughs."

Chicken Soup Analysis
Steve Roberts

During my hospital stay of twenty-eight days, I was drugged into a zone in which I didn't sleep or eat enough. I was going bonkers trying to keep my mind occupied during the long periods of lying awake. The challenge of summoning my strength to get out of bed to go to the bathroom was my highlighted relief. I developed mind games to help me pass the hours. One in particular helped me keep a spoonful of sanity.

At the insistence of the young dietician, I tried the hospital's chicken noodle soup. It seemed to be made by someone dedicated to making you swear off of soup the rest of your life. Images of Seinfeld's soup Nazi segment came to mind and seemed mild in comparison. Being a business consultant, I made a detailed cost analysis of the chicken noodle soup. I assumed that one chicken wing and one beak were used to make a day's batch of soup. Then I calculated that one egg and one gallon of flour were used for the noodles. On this basis, and assuming five percent of the unknowing patients ordered chicken noodle soup each day, there would be one four-inch noodle prepared for each serving of soup. As for water, I assumed the hose was put into the vat for four and a half minutes.

I held onto a chair as I wrote the financial analysis on the white board in my room. The next morning I carefully reviewed my findings with the whole band of medical people monitoring my case. I even asked the dietitian to stay after class for further insight and training. She smiled that smile that youngsters use on older citizens who are confused but well meaning. Then she left with the others.

I think perhaps the drugs and the lack of sleep had gotten to me.

Octowussy

Carol Larson

It had been a rough six weeks. I had entered the hospital June 1, 2006, for an operation to remove a cyst. Unfortunately, due to the fact I had colorectal cancer in 1999, my body was not as cooperative as it had been back then.

Due to radiation, I acquired a permanent ileostomy and a zillion of stringy adhesions in my intestines that made it impossible for the doctor to see the tree through the forest, you might say. It created even bigger problems for me, as I ended up with a perforated bowel, was put into a five-day coma, spent another week recovering from that, and now was sent to another hospital to rehabilitate for as long as it was going to take.

I didn't look so good after that. More like a sea creature with tentacles, although they were really cords attached to my IVs.

But I was finally feeling better. Lying in my hospital bed about 8:00 in the evening, propped up by a slanted back mattress and pillows, I started to relax.

I had people constantly attending me during my waking hours, and now I was deliciously alone, looking at the newspaper, planning what movie I wanted to watch on TV.

Except that the remote was missing. As well as I could, I rummaged through the bedcovers around me to find it, and then brumph—it fell on the floor.

Even though my arm was attached to an intravenous lifeline supplying me with nutrition, I determined that the cord would be long enough to allow me to get out of bed and retrieve my TV control apparatus.

I was correct. I slipped out of bed and sat down on the linoleum floor. Nothing went awry. No beeper announced any malfunction.

Trouble was, I didn't have the strength to get up again. I had been in bed for so long, and was so sick, my muscles had weakened. Standing up from a sitting position was the hardest task for me to do.

I reassessed the situation. Remote in hand. Body, okay. Was I in trouble? Nope. Not at all. Should I ring for the nurse? I didn't want to do that. I just got rid of her. That sounds terrible. I liked my nurses. A lot.

But it felt so good to be all alone.

So, I turned on the movie I selected and watched it for just a minute.

Then the phone rang. I thought about letting it go, but my daughters had been extremely protective of me lately and it might be one of them calling. I didn't want to cause them any unnecessary alarm. I reached up to my bed where I had left the phone and answered it.

"Mom?" Sure enough, it was Tami.

"Oh, hi," I said casually.

"How are you tonight?"

"Fine. I was just sitting here watching TV."

"Oh? What're you watching?"

"Ummm. A James Bond movie. I can't decide if I like Roger Moore better than Sean Connery."

There was a pause. Tami is like, psychic.

"Are you okay? You sound kind of out of breath."

"No, no, I'm just fine." But then, I couldn't think of anything more to say.

"Mom, what's going on? Where are you?"

"Well....actually, I'm on the floor." And then I explained my situation as well as I could.

"Omigosh, Mom. Should I be calling the desk?"

"No. Absolutely not. Honey, I'm not in trouble. If no one comes along, I'll ring the nurse."

Hooray. I knew at that moment I was taking charge of my life again. Tami wasn't sure this was a good thing, but she told me she would hang up and call back in five minutes.

And sure enough, two minutes later someone passed by my door, saw me on the floor, and helped me back into bed.

Tami called back and was relieved I was safely secured. I told her I definitely made up my mind. Sean Connery was better.

The Boney Hand

Carol Malzahn

I was in the hospital recovering from an emergency ileostomy surgery. My roommate was a spunky eighty-six-year-old woman who was recovering from hip replacement. One night I was sleeping, as good as one can in a hospital, and I lay half wake listening to a sound coming from my roommate. Thinking she was just trying to reposition herself in bed, I started to doze back off to sleep.

I awoke to some kind of rustling sound. I opened my eyes, and in my sleepy state, I saw an old wrinkled boney hand moving across the bottom of my bed. I barely held back a scream and started calling for help as well as pressing the nurse call button a dozen times. I thought, *either I am having a hallucinating nightmare from my meds or the* Dawn of the Dead *movies are real.*

My roommate had tried to get out of bed to go to the bathroom forgetting she had just had surgery. Instead of getting up, she slid to the floor and was feeling around for her call button. Needless to say I did not go back to sleep that night.

Glamour Shots
Diane Cannon

The time had come for me to get radiation markings to deal with cancer. I lay on the table with no clothes on from my waist down. I was fitted for a form that my legs would lay inside of. I had to put the bottoms of my feet together like a duck and let my legs lie flat, which was a feat in itself.

As with most cancer patients, I was in a daze and just let them do what was necessary. I received my six tattoos, one on each thigh, one in my pubic region that I couldn't see until my hair fell out, and the rest were on my butt, which I still can't see.

Then I had to have my picture taken—a crotch shot for my file. It was a week later that I went for my first radiation treatment. Still in my confused state, I went into the room and noticed that there was a file lying on the desk with a nude photo right on top of the file. I was immediately embarrassed for the poor soul who was radiated before me. I couldn't believe that the staff left this out for me to see, and I even questioned them about it. After all, I'm sure she signed the same HIPAA form I did.

It turned out that it wasn't the lady ahead of me; it was my own crotch I was seeing. Since I had never seen myself in this position, I was embarrassed, and yet at the same time, pretty impressed. I then asked if I could mass produce this picture, sell it online, and make enough money to pay for my treatment. They laughed. I was serious! After that, nothing embarrassed me.

The Godsend
Michael Mangano

I thought about the saying, *There are no atheists in foxholes*, and wondered how many atheists were in hospital rooms awaiting major surgery. Not very many, I figured. While I wouldn't say I was an atheist, I hadn't been a practicing Catholic for about forty years when the middle-aged, portly woman walked into my hospital room to ask if I'd like to receive communion before surgery. I thought it was a good idea, since if there was ever a time when I needed to be imbued with the body and blood of Christ, this was it.

Although I was an altar boy and attended parochial schools through college, I joined the lapsed Catholic coalition before Vatican II and was not well versed in the Church's current teachings. I asked the woman if it's alright these days to receive communion without having gone to confession. Looking as if I spoke a foreign language, she asked, "Would you like to see a priest?" For some time I had been contemplating having a conversation with a priest; there were several major issues I wanted to discuss. I figured if I could resolve them to my satisfaction, it might be an important step in my return to the church. "Yes, I would," I replied.

Unfortunately, the priest who visited only infuriated me. I asked him, "Can I receive communion without having gone to confession?"

"Well, you should go to confession at least once a year," he answered.

"I understand, but I'd like to receive communion now, before my operation, which is rather serious. It's a rare abdominal condition."

The priest responded, "You should try to get to confession at least once a year."

Not sure how to get through to him I asked, "Would you hear my confession now?"

"You can visit me at my parish in the future."

I thought, *I may not have a future, you idiot.*

Instead, I said, "Thank you very much," in a cool, dismissive way that also said, *Please leave.*

After he left, I wondered how this man of God could seem so uncaring, so ignorant of my condition and feelings. Fortunately, I didn't have time to spend obsessing over the experience; I was taken to the operating room immediately.

After the surgeon informed me of two courses of action we could follow, I chose the second, a surgery that was complex and would take about five hours, but would eliminate the risk of this condition returning. Making decisions of this magnitude in a matter of seconds isn't exactly my forte, but choosing the more precarious option (even without the benefit of communion) seemed the smarter thing to do.

Obviously, I survived the operation, but it was weeks before I was able to leave the hospital. I'm feeling pretty good these days, but continue to have unresolved religious issues and questions. Perhaps someday I'll have that conversation with a priest. Fortunately, and more importantly, the surgeon, who I later learned was one of the very best in the hospital, proved to be a godsend.

Who knows, maybe He really does work in mysterious ways.

Surprise Gifts

Heidi Dengrove

My surgery for colorectal cancer resulting in a colostomy, took place during the holidays. Everyone told me how sad it was that I had to be in the hospital for Christmas and my birthday, which was four days after Christmas; there would be no gifts. I didn't feel that way. I was there to get the best gift—a new life, being cancer free!

The surgery floor had lovely decorations. Due to fewer patients on the floor, it was especially peaceful. My bed near the window let me view colorful, sparkly city lights at night, even pretty snow showers. Walking the halls every morning, I saw each sunrise. How beautiful, what a gift to witness it.

Christmas morning, at the foot of my bed stood my surgeon to wish me a Merry Christmas. Four days later, first thing in the morning, there he was again to wish me a happy birthday! He remembered with no prompting or checking of the charts. He knew. He ordered a birthday cake especially for me. Even though I wasn't able to eat it, my husband took it home and froze it for me to enjoy later, but the thought was there!

Before I went home, the head of home nursing care visited to tell me I'd need a WOCN (Wound Ostomy Continent Nurse) for many weeks—and that I wouldn't have to worry about details or referrals, they would take care of it. What a gift that was. That was a Christmas with different gifts, the kind that last longest and mean the most.

Oh My God, I'm Catholic!

Lissa Brown

I almost became Catholic by accident when I was fifteen years old and a patient at Presbyterian Hospital. There's nothing wrong with being Catholic unless you are happy being from a Jewish family already.

The start of an uneventful summer after graduation from junior high school ended up in a way I never could have predicted. It was to be a summer of part-time work and part-time play. About to enter high school, I planned to spend the summer earning a few dollars to start my college fund.

The months leading up to ninth grade graduation were packed with school activities. I was burning the candle at both ends and nobody was too surprised that I was tired a lot of the time.

I joined my friend Jean and her family on a day trip to a lake a few days after school ended. We swam and played with a beach ball for hours and then ended the day at a tavern where her parents cooled off with a couple of beers while we played shuffleboard. By the time they dropped me off at our apartment, I was feeling the effects of a wicked sunburn.

My mother and brother were out and when I arrived home, I felt like I was on fire. Also feeling quite weak, I grabbed a box of frozen spinach from the freezer and put it on my forehead, figuring it would cool me down. I went to bed and remained there for a couple of hours until my mother returned. She looked at me, took my temperature, and tried to remain calm when she saw the reading of 108 degrees. She called an ambulance and started sponging me down with alcohol. Within minutes, I was being carried out of our apartment building on a stretcher, floating in and out of delirium.

The next few days blur in my memory, second-hand accounts tell of me being packed in ice to bring down my fever, while receiving intravenous fluids and having blood drawn. It seemed like a lot of fuss over sunburn to me, but I guessed the hospital staff knew what they were doing. I slept a lot and, at first, the only visitor I saw was my mother.

When I was re-hydrated and my fever broke, I became aware that I was quite sick. In tears, mother explained I was being tested for leukemia because my white blood count was abnormally high. I knew what leukemia was; a neighbor of ours had died from it when he was seven years old. Comic Red Skelton's son had just been diagnosed with it, and his parents were taking him on a world tour, presumably a final trip before his death.

"Will you take me to Europe?" I asked my mother. I thought it seemed an appropriate time for a wisecrack; somebody had to lighten up the conversation.

For six boring weeks while doctors tried to nail down a diagnosis, I rested away my summer in the hospital. I felt pretty good, just a bit tired. I ordered the complete works of Shakespeare from a mail order book supplier and worked my way through half of it. I also spent time figuring out how to escape the watchful eyes of the nursing staff so I could roam the hospital.

One afternoon I awakened from a nap to find a Catholic priest at my bedside setting up a tray with strange looking instruments and crackers.

"What are you doing?" I asked.

"I am preparing to give you Holy Communion," he answered.

"My mother will give you Holy Hell if you do—I'm Jewish!"

He looked at his patient list and realized he'd made a mistake.

"I apologize," he said and picked up his communion wafers and left.

Friends dropped by infrequently; the hospital was two bus rides from our neighborhood, and none of my friends were old enough to drive. A major problem in the hospital was that I couldn't get enough to eat. My poor mother had to stop en route to the hospital each evening after work to get me a sandwich since the hospital dietitian just wouldn't give me enough food. Inclined to be skinny by virtue of my genes, I was losing weight and nobody knew why.

After five weeks of inconclusive tests, my doctor stopped by.

"I am ordering another test." He went on to describe the test in vague terms. "It may be uncomfortable, but it is necessary to make the final determination of what is wrong with you."

I didn't know what to expect when four technicians showed up in my room the next day. Two of them looked like bouncers; they were needed to hold me down while someone drilled a hole in my chest and removed bone marrow from my sternum.

The technician showed me an instrument that resembled a corkscrew.

"I'm going to press down on your chest and steal a little of your bone marrow."

With panic growing inside me, I said, "I don't think I want this test done."

The next moment, the two bruisers were holding my arms and shoulders down in the bed. The fourth tech, a woman, was talking to me, trying to calm me down. I began kicking my legs, the only things beside my mouth I could still move. The talker became another bouncer and held my legs down.

"You'd better do it now," she told the woman with the corkscrew. I felt the sensation of someone squeezing the breath out of me. I heard the corkscrew grinding into my sternum and felt more and more pressure until there was nothing. I passed out.

I wasn't unconscious for more than a couple of minutes, and when I came to, the four people were still standing around the bed. I looked down at my chest and saw a large red cross.

"Oh my God, I'm Catholic," I screamed. "My mother's going to kill me. You turned me into a Catholic while I was passed out," I accused. They looked at one another in bewilderment, figuring I was crazy.

"Do you want to see a priest?" one of them asked me.

"No, I'm Jewish," I screamed.

"Calm down," the technician with the corkscrew said. "It's all over." She showed me a blob of bloody stuff in a test tube and said it was my bone marrow. By this time I was beside myself with anger at what I assumed was a forced conversion.

"Why did you put a cross on me?" I demanded.

All four of the technicians started to laugh. One of them pointed out, "That red cross on your chest is Merthiolate, it's routinely applied after the test to ward off infection. It has absolutely no religious significance."

I told them about the priest who had nearly given me Holy Communion as I slept a few days earlier and that I naturally thought when

I saw the cross on my chest that they'd been sent to complete what he could not.

A few days later my doctor arrived with the results of the bone marrow test.

"We've finally figured out what's wrong with you," he said. "You have mononucleosis, also known as the kissing disease. You don't have leukemia."

"S--t," I replied. "There goes my trip to Europe."

"You're going home tomorrow," he said. "You'll have to get to Europe some other way."

"Well, at least I'm still Jewish," I said and he walked out the door wondering what that meant.

Determination

Debby Reisinger

When a family member is in the hospital, the lives of the other family members are disrupted as well. They realize, however, they need to hold things together, and they usually perform admirably. I was quite proud of how I managed when my son, Jeff, was the victim of a hit and run accident. I shuttled between work and the hospital and remained on top of things. I admit that over time, there appeared a few cracks in my control.

One day, when the temperature was well below zero, I arrived at the hospital early in the morning and parked in the ramp. I left the hospital about noon to go to work, but I couldn't find my car. The ramp was only four levels and I walked it twice, my face and fingers stinging from the cold. My rational side told me the car had to be there, but I also knew I was very close to going to the security office, bursting into tears, and telling the officer my car was missing. Despite my mounting panic, I persuaded myself to do one more survey of the ramp and found the car inside the entrance where I had parked it.

Another day, I stopped for gas. I started fueling my car and went inside to pay where it was warm. After paying for the gas, I headed toward my car. A strange sound and the look on the face of another driver made me stop *immediately*. The gas nozzle was still attached inside the gas tank of my car but the hose was trailing along behind my car. Relieved to see that gas was not pouring from the pump, I released the nozzle, returned it to its niche and checked with the counter crew. They seemed unsure about what to do, so I told them I had left the hose at the pump and headed on my way. Something that on another day might seem like a big deal was, in the current context, a minor occurrence.

I realized extended family members were affected by Jeff's hospital stay, too. My son's cousin planned to visit him at the hospital. She decided to bring her four-year-old daughter, Ella, along. Apparently Ella had been warned about the possible dangers of being involved in an accident. Ella's mother explained they were bringing flowers to take along for the visit. It was obvious the mother left out an important detail when little Ella said to her, "Mom, your cousin that we're visiting—is he dead?" Satisfied with the explanation that Jeff was badly hurt, but not dead, Ella seemed to enjoy the visit, not at all intimidated by the bandages and medical equipment in Jeff's hospital room.

This story has a happy ending. A year later, Jeff is training for a half-triathlon—swimming, running, and biking. He is determined to finish with a great time to prove to himself and to his friends that he is fully recovered. And Ella. Ella continues to think deeply and to ask questions—it's a good way to learn.

Too Close for Comfort

Brenda Elsagher

I have talked to many people over the years that have faced the possible end to their lives because of a life threatening disease or they've had an event in life happen that changed them drastically, either physically or mentally.

I gave a presentation for a large gathering of people that had been diagnosed with multiple sclerosis (MS), were care givers or professionals that worked with people with MS. I relayed a story about just having been told by my doctor (whom I later referred to as the rear admiral) that I had a tumor or cancer, not just a hemorrhoid. Instantly I went into denial about cancer and, instead, focused on the fact that this doctor might be traumatized when he walked into that examination room seeing my large derrière sticking up in the air. I started panicking at the thought. *Is this the biggest butt this guy has ever seen? There was that one lady at the club… nope, I think mine is bigger.* Then, as a patient, I went on to rationalize. *Of course, he's seen a million butts; he can surely handle this one.* I was completely obsessed with the butt factor, not so much with the possible tumor.

After my presentation, a woman approached to talk to me. She was an acquaintance that I hadn't seen in fifteen years. Mary was at the conference because she struggled daily with MS. She went on to tell me how she related to my obsessive worry about my butt story.

"One day, I was walking along when my legs just gave out, and I fell down on the ground. I tried to get up to walk and I couldn't. A small group gathered around me and decided to call an ambulance. They were kind and stayed with me while we waited for the ambulance, very concerned for me. While they worried for me, all I could think about was, *why did I have to wear this stupid dress today of all days?* I knew I should have been worried about the fact that I couldn't walk, but as you were being obsessed with your butt, I was preoccupied by my dress."

You always hear that expression, *if you don't have your health, you have nothing.* I take exception to that. As a person who has come in and out of good health and knows many more like my friend Mary above, it's simply not true. Good health comes and goes, but if you don't have the love of family or friends or someone to love, *then* you have nothing. You'll find this to be true as you enjoy the following stories.

Prescription for Recovery
David Lang

As a physician, under the right circumstances, I find myself in a position to encourage my patients with my personal story. One recent patient was complaining about terrible neck pain and I wanted her to know how much I empathized with her, so I shared the following story.

On a Saturday night in September, I was on a fishing trip with several doctors and pharmaceutical reps in the northern woods of Wisconsin. Before dinner, we decided to relax in the hot tub, and afterward, we ran down the stairs to cool off in the lake. Two of my friends ahead of me led the way with resounding cannonballs and I followed right behind diving in, not realizing the water was only two-feet deep.

I felt my head strike the bottom and was immediately aware that I couldn't move a muscle and that I was floating face down. Oddly, I recalled no sense of panic, which I thought I would have, thinking I was about to drown. I was numb from the neck down and a realization came over me that things could be worse. I thought, *this is how I am going to die.* It wasn't painful; my spinal cord was shocked so I couldn't feel much of anything.

I didn't feel my friends' hands and arms turn me over. The next thing I knew is that I was staring up into the sky and had no clue how I had rolled over. One of my friends, a 250-pound former football player, cradled me with his arms as he picked me up out of the water and set me on the dock while the other physician friend guided my head and neck onto the dock so I wouldn't move it. They knew enough to stabilize my neck until the paramedics came and took me onto a stretcher to the local hospital.

While on the dock, I suffered a respiratory arrest cutting off my breathing ability while my heart kept beating normally. My lungs were temporarily paralyzed until my partner gave me the kiss of life. The mouth-to-mouth resuscitation saved me as the air filling my lungs helped the nerves get the signal going again to breathe on my own. The orthopedic surgeon friend came into the ambulance with me while the rest of them followed in the car.

I went into the emergency room and the first thing they did was take X-rays of my neck. My orthopedic friend told me I had broken two vertebrae in my neck, similar to the type of injury the actor Christopher Reeve suffered when he fell off his horse. By that point they had examined me, tested me, found my legs were working, and all my fingers were moving. It was a big relief. I wasn't paralyzed, and I would walk.

Soon after, I was put into temporary cervical traction where they put pins into my head attached to a weight that's connected to a pulley, which is a stabilizing treatment to keep my neck in place. I received a halo the next day. That halo is a steel circular band that has four bolts that were cranked down until they pierced my skin and drilled a hole into my skull; it's a sound that is horrifying. There are metal posts that get bolted into the halo and those go into a chest piece that confines you. It's so tight you can barely take a deep breath. It has to be tight enough that you can't wiggle your head.

Once in awhile I would panic, worried that I couldn't breathe, and then I took a valium. You have to sleep with the halo on, shower with it, and everything. It doesn't come off, it must be worn twenty-four hours a day, and I would periodically have to go in to tighten up the bolts that had loosened over time. Recovery took five months with the halo on before the bones were strong enough to take it off.

I was embarrassed by how stupid I was and yet I was resolved that the injury wasn't going to weaken me or keep me from doing anything I was accustomed to doing previously. One of my first thoughts along those lines was to return to ski the Birkibeiner, a thirty-five-mile cross country ski race in the upper part of Wisconsin that I had raced the previous ten years. During my recovery, I resolved to train again for this race after the halo came off. While I had the halo on, I rode a stationary bike almost every day, went for long walks, and lifted weights even though it hurt; I did take pain pills when necessary.

Six weeks later I was back to seeing patients, although I had to cut my doctor's coat so I could fit it over the halo device. My patients felt sorry for me and bad that they were complaining about minor things like their sore throats. I hated having to explain over and over what had happened, but no doubt it left an impression with them to be cautious about diving. Many of my patients were deeply moved and almost cried for me. I had felt that same way about them with their problems many times over the years as their physician, and now I was receiving empathy from them.

When I got the halo off, I still had to wear a hard plastic collar. Now I had eleven months to train for the cross country ski race. I upped my training with running increasing up to five miles at a time, four to five days a week, eventually training with a friend and entering smaller races while wearing the neck brace.

Initially, when the halo came off, my neck felt weak and as flexible as a rubber band because the muscles were atrophied, the hard collar aided in strengthening my neck; otherwise, I would not have been able to exercise. It took four more months before I no longer needed the stiff collar and my neck returned to have good strength. I was told it was 100 percent healed, and I wasn't going to let it make me a fearful person anymore.

Seven thousand people enter the Birkibeiner. The fastest skiers start at the beginning and then waves, depending on ability, took off. I started off in the last third of the pack. I wasn't sure how I'd be able to perform. It wasn't too far into the race when I felt confident that I'd be able to ski like I always could with my time done in about five hours. My wife and daughter waited for me at the finish line with tears in their eyes knowing what it took me to get that far. I had a celebratory unlit cigar in my mouth to show off at the finish line.

My patient listened to my story in awe and when she left that day, she thanked me for sharing my story and told me she felt inspired and knew that somehow she would get through her own pain too.

Bugs Behaving Badly
Paris Purnell

I worked as a nurse in a large metropolitan hospital in Sydney, Australia, in a very old ward for colorectal and upper gastrointestinal patients. We used to get a lot of extremely ill people straight from the intensive care unit who would require prolonged and difficult hospitalization. This can get very depressing for people who seem to have no date for getting home.

I had a long-term patient called Peter who was in isolation for an infection. He also had a tracheotomy, where the tube in the front of the neck aids in breathing. Peter had a long-term, life threatening illness and could get quite down at times.

One day I was in his room and Peter was pointing quite dramatically to this massive cockroach crawling on the floor. Sydney is well known for its large cockroaches that often fly in through the windows. In true football fashion, I raced after it and kicked it while it was in the corner. Needless to say it exploded up and all over my face and uniform. I could not freak out as Peter was laughing (silently because of the tracheostomy) so hard he almost went blue. It was wonderful to see him so joyfully laughing at my expense. I could only wipe it off and laugh with him, once he got his breath back.

Peter went home after several long months and I visited him afterwards—hale and hearty.

A Close Call
Rox Tarrant

I was raised in Alexandria, Minnesota, a small, midwestern city of ten thousand people. To say I lived a sheltered life was putting it mildly. The only crime I heard about was on the national or state news. I grew up believing that things happen for a reason, and I was pretty certain that my life would go according to plan.

After completing college, I spent a year as a VISTA volunteer (domestic Peace Corps) in Chicago. Quite a daunting task for someone growing up in a small town, but I believed I was on a path, an adventure with a challenge. I learned a lot, survived the big city of Chicago, and returned home to Minnesota.

After having lived for several years in the metropolitan city of Minneapolis, I was somewhat wiser, but not yet street savvy, when I found myself being in the wrong place at the wrong time. My girlfriend and I were leaving another friend's home one evening and had just gotten into my shiny, brand new, red 1982 Plymouth Horizon. An agitated man approached us and yelled, "Get out of the car!" I felt frozen, paralyzed with fear. I thought, *this only happens to other people.*

Another part of me was worried he was going to damage my new car. When we did not respond, he circled the car as if he was stalking his prey, then he walked to my friend on the passenger side and slammed the butt of the gun on the window, all the time yelling at us defiantly. There was commotion and noise outside of the car while inside we didn't move and couldn't react. It was slow motion as we watched this guy run around the car screaming, "Get out!"

Then, in frustration, he jumped onto the hood of my car, pointed his sawed off shotgun right at me through the windshield, and released the trigger. It was a moment in time that moved so quickly, yet seemed surreal to me. I kept thinking, *this is not happening to me.* Luckily for us, much of the blast was absorbed by my dashboard. All I could see was a smoky haze from the gunshot. If he had not been such a bad aim, I am certain I would not be alive today.

At least one hundred shotgun pellets hit me with a tremendous force. They struck me in my chest, my left arm, in my face, up my nose, dangerously close to my eyes and heart, narrowly preventing me from a life of blindness or death. My friend looked at me in horror as I was instantly bleeding profusely from my face while she escaped unharmed. In an instant, all the windows of my new car were blown out, the dashboard decimated, and hundreds of pellets impaled the interior.

The attempted robber jumped off the hood of my car and ran down the street. A nearby person in their home heard the shot and called 911. Within minutes, several police squads were there, along with an ambulance, and the sidewalks filled up with gawking people.

When I arrived at the hospital, they had to cut away my coat, my clothing, and then gave me numerous X-rays to make sure the pellets had not punctured vital organs. I was in a lot of pain, glass was in my eyes, my arms were swollen, and my nose hurt badly. This happened to me around 8:00 p.m. and my mother saw my car and heard about it on the ten o'clock news that same evening. My girlfriend and boyfriend stayed by my side in the hospital.

I remained hospitalized for a week in a state of shock. I developed post traumatic stress disorder, and it took months of therapy to regain my self confidence and to be able to walk down the street without feeling afraid. As the wounds healed and weeks passed, people stopped asking me about the event, but I never forgot it.

I am certain it was God's grace that saved me that night, and I never gave up hope that I would return to my old self again—someone who laughed easily and who thought most people were inherently good. I returned to Alexandria to be cared for by my mother for a couple of weeks while my wounds healed until I was ready to return to my home. It took a while before I relished the idea of being alone once again and my self confidence restored.

The man that shot me was apprehended within hours and placed in jail. He pleaded not guilty, and we attempted to bring it to trial over a period of nine months and I couldn't get closure. Finally on the day he was supposed to go to trial, he pled guilty. There was a pre-sentence hearing that the judge invited me to attend, hoping to help me move on with my life. I had written a letter, and I told the judge how difficult it had been for me.

He appreciated my letter and wasn't going to impose restitution because he thought it was hopeless with this man, but he wanted to wish me the best. I got to see the man who assaulted me, and it struck me that he was only nineteen years old and that in the room that day was his seventeen-year-old girlfriend and two-year-old baby. I thought, *what a waste of a life and for what? It all seemed so senseless to me.* The experience helped me move on once I was acknowledged.

That terrifying ordeal taught me so much about myself. I discovered that I had much more potential than I ever dreamed and nothing could hold me back from doing what I wanted in my life. It didn't taint my life. I felt like I had a second chance and that I didn't want to take things for granted. I was given an opportunity to be in this world and to make a difference. I went from an impressionable young woman who lived a sheltered existence to a woman who could tackle things in her life, anything she wanted to do. Out of this dark time, there emerged much lightness to my life. I still believe things happen for a reason.

Ever on the Job
Cheryl Jobe

The occurrence of childhood kidney disease had damaged both kidneys and my liver. I had known that at some time problems could resurface. I would never have suspected the awakening of a second and more severe bout of disease could bring me so low.

Thankfully, for much of the long illness I was in a coma, spared the worry and pain my loved ones endured. It is confusing to become aware that not only have you been absent from yourself for a period of time, but many things have happened or been done to you. Those who *were* there are understandably reluctant, for their own sake as well as yours, to clue you in on what you missed and they experienced.

After six weeks, the doctors released me from the intensive care unit and I was sent to a hospital for critical care patients. After that, I went to a nursing home for respiratory and physical therapy. I was in a muddle of memory loss and illness, yet anxious to get on my feet and return to my life. It was an eye opening experience and one I'll never forget nor regret.

I had been raised among elderly people; my grandparents had children at an older age, so I was comfortable in the midst of elders. While my parents worked, my long-retired grandfather had been my caretaker through the childhood disease, thus it seemed natural to be where I was. The first ten days, I had a nasal tube for feeding, a leftover from the hospital that I could not be free of until my throat muscles became strong enough for proper swallowing. Anyone who thinks seniors are stodgy and humorless have much to learn. I endured much good natured teasing about my "trunk" and endless giggles.

One evening, the tube had become dislodged and when the nurse on duty reinserted it, there was some doubt that it had been placed correctly. A gurgling noise should be heard through the stomach wall if done properly. If there were no sounds, the danger would be of it entering the bronchial passage instead and the fluid would fill my lungs. I knew I was in the best hands with a wonderful nurse, an older lady, who looked forward to retirement, and who had the wisdom and patience from years of experience. There would be no liquid food until an X-ray could be taken to check the placement. It was late on a Sunday night and a machine had to be brought from a town thirty miles away. Unfortunately, the technician with the van and equipment was at another location an equal distance in the opposite direction. We tried to stay calm, hoping he'd be there soon. When he arrived, he would take the X-ray, return to the lab, and call when the film was developed. Bad weather slowed his progress, but eventually he arrived, the picture was taken, and we began the wait for results.

With no liquid feeding for several hours, my blood sugar dropped sharply while the nurse went to check on another patient. My husband brought Life Savers for me to suck on when my mouth was dry. On instinct, he retrieved the hidden candy and gave me a piece. When the nurse returned she tested the sugar levels and agreed, "That was quick thinking; it's what I would have done."

I needed more than one piece or a shot of insulin would soon be required to prevent diabetic shock. Admittedly, I wasn't disappointed to actually taste something, either. In pain, I anxiously awaited the phone call.

The caring nurse declared, "There's nothing else *we* can do, we need to…pray!"

As we joined hands, she led us in a brief, confident prayer for our situation to be resolved, pledging our trust in the Almighty. Less than ten minutes later, the report came in; everything was fine and the fluid and medication were re-administered. Before she left the room, I held my hand out to her and my husband, "We need a moment to thank the One who answered our prayer of desperation." A miracle had been granted, and we saw clearly the effect of prayer in action.

Over the course of my lifetime I have known several such instances, with others or me—situations that are beyond man, medicine, or seemingly beyond hope. But in faith and prayer lies the answer. Many times the greatest lessons are learned not through the best events in our lives, but through the worst. Even in the depths of a coma, I had been touched by the prayers of loved ones, both family and friends.

That lovely nurse has retired, and I still visit the nursing home from time to time. Many of my friends have left for their new home. A chat is welcomed by almost any resident, so new friends are quickly and easily made. Although I was in the home for a much shorter stay than most, I know there is love and true caring in many of these places of temporary rest. The Lord is on the job in all; he wears many faces and has many tasks.

Catch of the Day
Carol McAdoo Rehme

A phone call.

A plane ride.

A race to the hospital.

I still shudder at the thought. I had come so close to losing Kyle. Although he wasn't out of the woods yet, at least he was stabilized. At least he was still alive. In the meantime, my life settled into a routine of its own. A simple breakfast, a ninety-minute drive, and each day spent visiting the care unit to spend time with my twenty-two-year-old son before the long drive home at night.

During the coma, pneumonias attacked his lungs, infections invaded his blood, and bed sores appeared in odd places. On the other hand, while he was asleep, his cracked ribs healed, his lungs re-inflated, and his crushed leg accepted the titanium rod. Now that he was awake and alert, I fretted over the wait-and-see outcome of his severe head trauma.

Early on, I had hardly recognized my son. Kyle was like a voodoo doll. Needles, wires, and catheters pierced him. Hoses shackled him. Tubes and cords crisscrossed his body like a fishing net. It felt odd to see him prone, horizontal, still.

Before this hit-and-run biking accident, nothing about Kyle was still. He was as lively as one of the trout on his stringer, busy flipping and flopping between one activity and the next. In fact, fishing counted among his other outdoor hobbies of archery and camping. He roamed the foothills of Colorado's Front Range and hunted the Rockies for signs of elk and deer, hoping for a rare glimpse of moose. And, of course, he tossed the occasional line into icy mountain rivers, looking for relaxation along with a skillet of fish to cook over his campfire for supper.

Kyle was handling his hospitalization better than I was. Those first tenuous hours melted into days and the days into weeks. Dark circles ringed my eyes, worry lines gridded my forehead, and clothes hung on my too-thin frame. I was exhausted, utterly worn down. Kyle noticed. I could tell. Now *he* was worrying about *me*.

Today was different.

Even before the elevator doors slid fully open, I heard it—laughter. Laughter?

Oh, it wasn't the stilted laughter of awkward visitors. It wasn't even the brittle laughter born of tension. It was real laughter, from the belly, and it was coming from Kyle's room.

I paused at the threshold, hardly believing my ears and eyes. The room pulsed with more than the beeps of monitors. It throbbed with the life that only laughter brings. And it was due to Liam, a new nurse.

His was a one-man comedy routine. He cast out snappy jokes, witty one-liners, and rib-tickling stories. Not only was Kyle actually smiling, so was the small crowd of staff that had collected to provide an avid audience and to egg Liam on while he reeled in everyone with his nonsense.

My initial reaction was indignation. *How dare he? Didn't this cocky male nurse know the seriousness of Kyle's condition? Didn't he understand how to act in a hospital room?*

As I paused in frustration, I looked towards my son and witnessed a slow smile spread across his face and widen until it erupted into a full-fledged grin. His golden eyes were bright as they met mine. I could see his own quick wit itching to toss out a few quips of his own. I knew that, if it weren't for the tracheotomy at the base of his throat, he would be matching Liam joke for joke. Suddenly, for the first time in weeks, my own spirits lightened and lifted with hope.

I, too, found myself responding to the gags and tales. It dawned on me that Liam's vivaciousness, his optimism, and his contagious cheer weren't an intrusion; they were antidotes, good medicine. A clear reminder that life has its joyous moments, too.

Thanks to Liam's example, I learned a valuable lesson: I learned that humor heals—hook, line, and sinker.

Heart-Stopping Action
Paris Purnell

Winding down from my long evening shift as a nurse, we turned the lights off and darkness and quiet settled comfortably over the ward. The shift changeover was due soon, and we were enjoying a peaceful, relaxing moment until someone from the darkness started screaming for a nurse.

My colleague and I raced into the darkness to assist. I was moving lightning fast—so fast that I could literally feel the air moving around my head on the way to the rescue. We quickly got the collapsed patient onto the bed and resuscitated him. He was saved and moved to an intensive care unit for further treatment.

On the way back, I noticed my colleague, in her rush ahead of me, had literally jumped out of her shoes. Then I realized it wasn't air that had flown past each side of my head. With our minds at the crisis before us, I never noticed her giving cardiac compressions in her bare feet. We found her shoes on the floor near the office—a long distance from the patient.

The Mysterious Malady—Measles
Annette Geroy

My jaw hung slack and my mouth went mute as my mind screamed, *Let me go get the medical book!* The young ER doctor had just mumbled those words, embarrassed to acknowledge he was at a loss while facing a frustrated mother who insisted on a diagnosis. The myth that doctors know everything died a slow death as my gaze shifted to our young daughter. Lethargy and another spiked fever indicated the seriousness of her condition.

The doctor walked back into the room, gazed down as he flipped through *the book.*

"Measles. Measles. I have never seen a case of measles. Did she have a measles vaccination?" he asked for the third time.

"Yes!" I declared a little too emphatically. "But I had the measles when I was twelve and I think that is what she has now."

Those words earned me an unrestrained scowl from the infant doctor. Unfortunately, I was too desperate to care that it made him uncomfortable.

This was our third doctor's visit in five days and our child's condition was only getting worse.

Our young family doctor had declared chicken pox, and sent us home with Tylenol and instructions to watch for more eruptions. Even though we continued to report periodic spikes of fever and splotchy red rashes over the next two days, she still insisted we wait it out because she was sure it was chicken pox. We waited. Who was I to question her diagnosis?

I finally decided to try a medical emergency clinic. After all, it was now the weekend. This doctor, not so young, examined our daughter's throat, saw splotches there, and declared strep throat. As if on cue, Ginny's fever had gone down and the red rash had disappeared by the time we got to the clinic. When I asked about the possibility of measles, he said, "Kids don't have measles anymore. Vaccinations, you know, have taken care of the big three—measles, mumps, rubella. The fever and rashes can be symptomatic of strep throat."

But he didn't want to use a targeted antibiotic until the report on the throat culture came back. That would take several days—since it was the weekend. He sent us home with Tylenol and a prescription for a generic antibiotic. I still was unconvinced, but he was the doctor. Right?

Ginny's fever rose to dangerous levels over the next twenty-four hours, so Sunday afternoon we finally took her to the emergency room.

And now the doctor was saying, "Let me go get the medical book."

The book seemed to verify my suspected diagnosis. Measles—a respiratory disease caused by a virus that normally grows in the cells that line the back of the throat and in the cells that line the lungs. The symptoms of measles include a rash, high fever, cough, runny nose, and red watery eyes, which are sensitive to light. She was admitted to the hospital.

By this time, Ginny's throat was almost closed due to swelling, and she was having difficulty breathing. The swelling was so severe that a tracheotomy was ordered. After several terrifying moments, an ear-nose-throat specialist showed up with the suggestion that they try a Tylenol/Benadryl/Maalox gargle first. She was to gargle with the liquid mixture every two hours, then swallow. Thankfully it worked, soothing the swollen passages and lulling her into a restful sleep.

Ginny was in the hospital a full week. During that time, all of the ER staff and pediatric nurses received gamma globulin injections to boost their immunity to the virus. Because the measles virus is highly contagious, the eight hundred students and staff in her middle school also received booster shots. Much to her chagrin, by the time she returned to school, simply everyone knew her name!

Being the patient who stumped the doctors brought its own notoriety. Ginny's strawberry blond hair and freckled ivory complexion made her the perfect poster child for a classic case of measles. Like the young ER doctor, many of those on the hospital staff had never seen the measles. They all stopped by, paying curious homage, to check her out. Each visitor stepped into the darkened room with mouths masked, hands behind their backs. The pediatric nurses were so helpful and attentive throughout the week that we felt like family by the time we left.

So how did this happen? Vaccination against measles should be administered on or after the first birthday, two doses separated by twenty-eight days or more. Ginny was vaccinated before her first birthday—during a time when her body was not prepared to produce the necessary antibodies. Actually, there was a large outbreak of measles that year, allowing the medical community to document the reasons: a weak vaccine for some and early inoculation for others.

Measles spreads so easily that anyone who is not immunized is susceptible to infection. Complications from this virus can include diarrhea, ear infections, pneumonia, encephalitis, seizures, and death. In developing countries, outbreaks of measles have been known to kill as many as one out of four people. It is documented as the leading cause of blindness among African children. Even in today's world of sophisticated vaccines and improved hygiene, measles kill almost one million children each year.

It is scary to realize how close we came to losing Ginny because the doctors would not listen to us. It was frustrating because we had to second guess our gut feelings that things were not right. Our persistence turned out to be not only important, but imperative. We applaud the young ER doctor for not being too proud to go get the medical book. He probably saved our daughter's life.

The $3,000 Stone

Carole Turner

As much as I enjoy traveling, I have found it best to be reasonably healthy when doing so because it can be rather upsetting and costly to require medical attention away from home and "out of network." The phrase "out of network" is insurance jargon for, "This ER visit will require you to take out a second mortgage," or "This ten-minute procedure will cost more than your last car."

Recently, while cruising up the Mississippi on board a large riverboat, my husband awakened during the night in severe pain. He was violently ill and nauseated. With unsteady hands, I dialed the Purser's Office, and they promptly dispatched an EMT who took my husband's vitals and asked several questions about symptoms and medical history. The EMT encouraged my husband to drink as much water as he could and to rest. He promised to return later.

My husband slipped in and out of consciousness so easily, it was frightening. He moaned and writhed in pain when awake, then dropped quickly into a deep sleep that seemed to border on comatose. There we were, out on the legendary Mississippi, several hours from our next port of call, and very far from home. All kinds of concerns, none of them pleasant, raced through my sleep-deprived mind. *What is the matter, and how serious is it?* was my most frequent thought.

After speaking by cell phone to medical experts somewhere on shore, the EMT returned with the news that an ambulance would meet the boat when it docked later in the morning. The phrase "in sickness and in health" crossed my mind occasionally, and I wondered what the day would bring. After we docked, an ambulance crew crowded into our tiny cabin, placed my husband on a gurney, and off we went. Since my husband's pain had eased a bit and he was not in apparent danger, the ambulance proceeded through the streets of the quiet little river town at a normal speed without sirens.

Soon we arrived at a small community hospital whose name I distinctly recall seeing on the ER doors—Out of Network Hospital. After a thorough examination, the ER doctor opined that perhaps diverticulitis might be the culprit, and diagnostic tests would be necessary. The nurse administered an IV drip containing pain medication, which eased my husband's discomfort considerably. He began entertaining the ER staff with jokes and almost seemed to be enjoying himself. During the next ninety minutes, he sipped down three large styrofoam containers of contrast medium, and then was transported to nuclear medicine for tests.

Before long, we had the answer to the medical mystery that had turned our vacation topsy turvy—kidney stones. No surgery or hospital stay was required. The doctor assured us that there was no need for concern. The stones were small, and they would pass easily with an assist from the pain medication and plenty of water.

We took a cab back to the dock and boarded the riverboat shortly before it departed on the final portion of the cruise. The remainder of our trip was pleasant and uneventful.

Though our medical insurance did cover some expenses, our share was considerably more than the cost of the cruise. Moral of the story: Don't travel with a traveling kidney stone. Stay home or close to home, preferably in the same time zone—and in network. Oh, and be sure to drink plenty of water.

Breast Assured

Brenda Elsagher

Five years after I was diagnosed with colorectal cancer, my mother got the news she had breast cancer. After a lumpectomy and radiation, she is doing great. Four years later, my sister Laurie was given a diagnosis of breast cancer, too. Her treatment required a lumpectomy, chemotherapy, and radiation. It has been almost five years now, and she is doing well also.

Since I came from a family that includes seven daughters, it is natural to think more often of the possibilities of getting breast cancer. My sisters and I are all aware of the importance of mammograms and early detection. I've had so many mammograms done now that I used to be a 42 C, now I'm a 46 long. But, rest assured, these stories won't leave you long in the face; read on and prepare to smile.

Amusing Mother

Jon Eveslage

A couple years ago, my eighty-five-year-old mother fell down and broke three ribs and punctured a lung. While Mom was recuperating in the hospital, the nurse would take her for walks to help her regain her strength. One time, Mom was having a little trouble with her breathing, so the nurse said, "It helps if you have big breaths."

Mom replied, "Well, when I was younger, I was a thirty-eight!"

Another time, Mom was playing Balderdash with us and the word was "titubating." It means, "to walk with a limp" and Mom thought it was the funniest word. She'd had her hip replaced, so she told her friends, "My hip aches today, so I'm titubating!"

A Legend at Nursing School

Avamarie Miller

We froze when through the door strolled hair the color of winter wheat, eyes Caribbean blue on a day without waves, and oh yeah, biceps—the size of cantaloupes. My school offered blood pressure screening to the community, so we rookie nursing students could practice on unsuspecting victims.

"Take a seat," my instructor told the walking romance cover, while nudging me forward. Like a cobra she hissed in my ear, "Don't mess up, again!" I guess she hadn't forgotten last week's enema fiasco and dropping the patient's dentures in her bed pan *was* purely an accident.

My hands shook—taking this hotter than a Texas summer's blood pressure wasn't going to be easy. I had to stretch across the wide table to wrap the black cuff around the cantaloupe of steel. Following my instructor's rule, I extended the patient's arm with palm up. Peeking at Adonis, I added my own rule—no drooling. I put the stethoscope on his pulse and heard our hearts beat as one. I inflated the cuff and felt the planets align in the universe. Chancing a look at my possible happily ever after, I saw shock and confusion on his face and beads of perspiration forming on his forehead. Exhaling, he forced his breath through those kissable lips and whistled like an overheated tea kettle. To calm him, I gave my best reassuring student nurse smile, hoping he couldn't read my thoughts. *I want to be your baby's momma!* I released the cuff's pressure and his pulse pounded in my ears like a jackhammer bingeing on caffeine.

Yikes! I didn't expect those numbers from my fantasized husband. His handsome, hypertensive face hypnotized me and zombie-like I said, "You need to see a doctor for your high blood pressure," I said as I silently called dibs on the mouth-to-mouth part if he had a heart attack.

"Take it again." A grin covered his face like a Cheshire cat guarding a secret. "It'll be lower, I promise."

Beneath his chiseled cheekbones, sparkling dental perfection blinded me. Close to breaking my no drool rule, I could only nod. With my brain-to-mouth connection out of order, I'd lost the ability to form words as I drowned in his Caribbean blues.

As he took a slow, deliberate look down his cuffed arm to where my body draped across the table, I heard my instructor gasp. Then my Adonis winked and spoke the words that secured my place of infamy at nursing school, "Take my blood pressure again…but this time, can you do it without your boob resting in my hand?"

The Breast Exam
Alanna Seppelt

When I was a student years ago, I was doing my first health and physical examination on a nursing home resident. My instructor stood in on the assessment to grade my skills. I did a chart review prior to doing the exam and read that the lady had a unilateral mastectomy. It is said that when a female has a mastectomy, you are still supposed to do a breast exam as if they still had one. When I opened up the gown to do my exam, I was quite surprised to see that she had a bilateral mastectomy, and I even commented on this to my instructor.

I thought I had done a thorough chart review. I did not let this stop me, so I examined both as if she had breasts. I then went to turn my lady over to do an examination of her backside. It was at this time that her right breast came swinging around. It had such a sag to it that the breast was flat to the side and tucked under my little lady. It was a fast way to learn that not all breasts show up right away.

Mammogram Musings
Mia Probst

Since I give mammograms, there are many times when a patient will ask, "Is this what you do all day?" Because I know how important mammograms are, I usually say, "Yes, I help save lives." But as important as it is, I personally still enjoy the humor of some people's reactions to what is a unique situation.

When I was being trained in positioning mammograms, the tech told me about one of her patients who told her that the mammogram machine was the "original booby trap." Some people feel the need to comment on their own anatomy and it was still early on in my career doing mammogram examinations when I brought a patient into the room who said, "What do you do with a couple of fried eggs?" My mouth dropped open when I realized what she referred to; it was the first time I had ever heard that statement. But not the last. She followed up with, "If I had a lump in these breasts I would certainly know!"

One time while placing a little grandma for her mammogram she said, "These used to be so important when I was young, but now they are just something to lift up and wash under!" Some patients are leery of getting radiation. I was using a machine that had the letters AEC, which stood for "Automatic Exposure Control." While I was situating the patient, I could tell she didn't want any X-radiation, and then she commented, "I haven't seen that abbreviation for a long time." I was curious to know what she thought those letters stood for, so I asked her and she responded, "Atomic Energy Commission." I assured her nothing would glow after her mammogram.

One morning I asked the patient her medical history before doing the exam. She was sitting in front of me with her hospital gown wide open exposing her chest. Most people are quite shy about exposing themselves and wait until the last possible minute to disrobe, so I was a little taken aback. She must have sensed that I was uncomfortable because just then she told me that she belongs to a nudist farm. There is a first time for everything!

A Breastfeeding Failure
Judy Epstein

I was a failure. Sitting on the living room couch, my pajama top open and the blinds drawn at four in the afternoon, my baby and I were both crying hysterically. Tears rolled down my face and dripped onto his, cradled next to breasts, which apparently did not work.

"What good is it if I can't even feed my baby?" I wailed. "It's supposed to be so simple—cows can do it!" But not, apparently, me.

I had tried and tried, and so had my baby—on our own, with experts, and with awkward, bulky equipment—and we were both getting nowhere. Only thirty days a mother, I had failed him at the most basic level: mother's milk.

I stood at a fork in the road. One choice was recommended by all the experts as the best for my child; the other was the one I was about to take. I kept hearing these lines from Robert Frost's poem: *"I took the one [road] less traveled by, And that has made all the difference."* What if it *did* make all the difference and the road I chose was the wrong one?

This was not what I'd planned. I had always been on good terms with my breasts. They had gotten me plenty of dates in high school, and it made sense to think they'd work as God had intended.

I wanted to breastfeed. I bought all the theories: it's the easiest option—no bottles to make or sterilize; the cheapest—no formula to buy; the healthiest—every antibody and nutrient your baby needs, miraculously blended to suit every stage of their life. And it's psychologically best for you both as well; just clap baby to bosom and bond.

There are just a few things the theories left out.

It isn't easy.

You have no idea what you're doing. Here's the primal breast-feeding scene: New mother nurses baby. Total stranger walks in and asks, "Is the baby getting enough?" New mother then goes ballistic, as this is precisely what she has spent the last twenty-four sleepless hours panicking about already.

It hurts like hell! My toothless infant, six hours old, clamped down on my nipples hard enough to make me scream, then began sucking hard enough to give me hickeys. Over the next few days my nipples cracked so badly they bled. Convinced this was horribly wrong, I rang for the lactation consultant. She assured me, "If you can uncurl your toes after the first thirty seconds, you're doing it right."

Best of all, you must repeat the process every two hours—around the clock.

Of course, my baby and I had had more than our share of troubles. At two days of age, he developed jaundice, which kept him in the hospital under lights (and needing extra milk) while I was sent home without him. At home, I developed a high fever that put me back in the hospital (intensive care) for a week, and *he* went home without *me*. Then, two days after I went home for the second time, he got a fever that returned him to the hospital. The emergency room nurse said, "You again?"

It was like a Marx Brothers movie, *A Month at the Hospital.*

All told, my baby and I had been together only eight of his first twenty-one days. I had rented a breast pump to use during my ICU stay, but it wasn't enough (I had foolishly chosen to sleep some of the time, instead). So by the time we got back together, his demand for milk was zooming just as my supply was packing it in.

On to another consultant who told me both that I was not making enough milk, and that the baby didn't suck correctly. The most basic instinct for all mammals, but somehow he was doing it wrong. To correct both problems, I was to wear a contraption every time I nursed, hanging a flask of formula around my neck with two angel-hair-pasta-sized tubes leading from it, taped to myself so the ends stuck out just beyond my nipples. It reminded me of those beer hats guys wear to baseball games—except *I* was the beer and the hat. My first try was a disaster. My second try was even worse.

Whose idea was this? Nine months of increasing sleeplessness and pain, capped off by labor, or surgery, or for those lucky few, both; then, just when you could sleep for a week, you have to *breastfeed.*

For me, this is sufficient proof that God is not a woman. In fact, I asked Him about this very question.

"Why *us*, Lord? We carried the weight, swelled up, and had to watch every blessed thing that went into our bodies for nine long months. Why can't the men take a turn? Why not give them the breasts?"

He answered, "You know what I had to work with. I couldn't always count on them to still be around when the baby's born."

I was not impressed. "So? You're Omnipotent; why not *make* them be there?"

But apparently God, like everyone else, believes that if you want something done, give it to a busy woman.

It's just so improbable. Everything else that comes out of your body, you get rid of as quickly and hygienically as possible; this, you give to your baby. Breastfeeding was the biggest disappointment in my life—worse than finding out that the chocolate Easter bunny is hollow.

It didn't help that public opinion was virtually monolithic. Never have I encountered such unanimity! Every book, every article, even the back of the formula can, for heaven's sake, started the same way: *Of course, breastfeeding is best. But....* It didn't matter what they said after that. I knew what they meant: *But if you don't care what happens to your baby, go right ahead.*

The truth was I didn't have much choice. Still, I couldn't face it. I felt so horrendously guilty.

Sitting in that darkened living room, all I could see were scenes of my baby's ruined future. He's six months old. We're at the mall. He's screaming with hunger while I rummage through the diaper bag, desperate, because I'd left all the bottles home. Two years later, he's the clingiest kid in playgroup, a pacifier dangling from his lips night and day because he never got enough oral gratification. Or the same scene, twelve years later, except the pacifier is now a cigarette—and all because on this day in his young life, I couldn't take it anymore.

I wanted to scream with anger, misery, and frustration. But someone else was already doing that, and I was supposed to be the grown-up in the room. I took off the harness and went to warm up a bottle.

It was such a relief, knowing he was getting enough to drink. And our relationship instantly felt healthier. My breasts shrank back to being just part of my anatomy. Feeding him became just one of many things I did, along with burping him, changing him—oh, and *playing* with him—all things I hadn't even thought about before. I had been so fixated on the baby in those dismal futures that I couldn't see the one right in front of me. I forgot that *he* might have other needs, even if I decided I didn't. It wasn't until I gave up on breastfeeding and went to bottles that I realized he might be crying because he was wet, lonely, or bored, and not for my breast at all.

Turns out that fork in the road wasn't Robert Frost's after all. It's more like one near my house where it doesn't matter which road you take because they come back together, two blocks down. After eighteen months, I can see the differences erasing between me and the breastfeeding moms, as we all try to wean our babies to cups. Maybe I even have an edge; for me, it's just a bottle versus cup—it's nothing personal.

As for convenience, I did have to wash a lot of rubber nipples, but I never forgot his bottles, and they had a convenience of their own. I could feed him in his car seat without pulling over. When I splurged and met friends for lunch, I could leave him in his stroller and hold his bottle with one hand while eating my own pre-cut meal with the other.

Best of all, when he comes running now and asks me to pick him up, I know it's not because I'm dinner. Even if he does ask me to open the refrigerator and get him a cup of milk!

CHAPTER 4

Worthwhile Work

Brenda Elsagher

I was giving a talk a couple of years ago for a roomful of nurses in Minneapolis who were trained to work with patients that required wound, ostomy, or continent care (WOCN). I told them that patients never forget the face of those special nurses who cared for us when we were at our most vulnerable. (Unless you're high on morphine, but then you can't help that.) I looked around the room and said that I didn't see the nurse that came to teach me about working with my ostomy or I'd know her. Just then, a head popped out from behind someone and I pointed at her and said, "It was you." At first I had the hospital wrong, (there have been a few too many) where I met her, but we straightened it out and I realized it really was her. I proved my point and it had been twelve years since I had seen Terri.

She wouldn't remember me because she'd seen thousands of patients since me, and I teased her that she didn't recognize me without my hospital gown on, not to mention the fact that I was standing up. When I think back on the day I met her, I didn't respond too well to what she was telling me. I wasn't prepared to deal with my colostomy when I had a multitude of other physical problems to adjust to at that same time. But she pushed on, continuing to educate me on how to take care of myself. I am sure she thought I didn't take in anything she said, but when the time came that I had to care for my ostomy on my own, her words came back to me.

She came up to me afterward and I gave her a hug and offered her a long overdue thanks. Her job was important to me, and she was good at her work. You'll find many people in the following chapter that find their work with patients worthwhile too.

To Go Bag
Susan Pawlak

My shift was over. It was time to go home. The trek to the parking lot was a long one, and it was pouring rain. My umbrella was conveniently located in the trunk of my car.

I decided to grab a plastic bag out of the closest linen cart and drape it over my head. It was pretty large, so I thought, *Great. I'll be fairly dry by the time I get to my car.*

The rain was coming down really hard and the wind was blowing, so even with my trusty plastic bag I decided to make a mad dash for it. However, the closer I got to my car, the smaller the bag got. *What the heck?*

By the time I got to my car, I was soaked, and the bag had shrunk to the size of table napkin. It turns out I had grabbed a bag used for isolation linens. The bags were made from a gel-type material that dissolved when the bag with the linens in it were put into the washing machine.

Hannah
Pamela Goldstein

Hannah was 106 years old, tiny in stature, frail as a sparrow, and toothless. She was a proud woman and she held her head high with nobility the likes of which I had never seen, not even in Queen Elizabeth. She was in the hospital for a small stroke she'd had on an Easter Sunday.

That was forty years ago. I remember her as if it were yesterday.

"I was the first one in my family to have an education," Hannah told me. "I became a teacher. Could never teach in a white school, though. Had to wait until I moved here to Canada."

"Where are you from?" I asked.

"Born and raised in Georgia I was, during the American Civil War. My ma and pa and me were slaves until that war ended. I was seven years old at the time."

"Wow, you lived through that war?" I said while placing a cup of tea in front of her. Hannah loved afternoon tea with cookies, the vanilla ones with strawberry jam centers.

"I surely did, child. None of my brothers survived, but I never knew them well. They had been sold to a farmer down the road when I was still a baby."

"What do you remember about that time, Hannah?"

Hannah shrugged her shoulders. "Nothin' much, other than bein' hungry." She smiled. "But I do remember one day in particular. The day I met President Abraham Lincoln."

I plopped down in the chair next to her. "You met Abraham Lincoln? What was he like?"

"Oh, my. Well, he was a very tall man. Thin but broad shoulders. Kinda ugly, actually, and he had bad teeth. But there was somethin' wonderful about him. He had kind eyes. You could tell from just lookin' at him that he was a wise man."

She took a sip of tea. "I didn't talk to him long, maybe a minute or two. But I'll never forget what he said to me. He said, 'Be proud, child. Always be proud of who you are and where your family came from. There's no shame in having been a slave. But you're free now, and it's your responsibility as a free person to do good in the world.' I believed him."

She looked down at her hands. "I told all of my students what President Lincoln said that day, and I made them promise to be responsible free people and to do good. And I believe they all did. Except for that Randy Smith. He was a no-goodnik from the get go, that boy was. It didn't surprise me a bit when he was charged with murder."

"I'm shocked you remember what Mr. Lincoln said to you, Hannah," I said, trying not to laugh at her little outburst of annoyance at Randy Smith. "I don't remember anything anyone said to me when I was seven."

"But you never met President Lincoln, child. Like I said, there was somethin' about him."

She winked. "Besides, I had a permanent mark to remember him by."

"What?"

She held up her right hand. It was completely white from the skin disease vitiligo. "This hand. It's the one he shook. And right after he shook it, the darn thing turned white as snow. I swear it was a sign from the Lord above to never forget President Lincoln's words. And with a powerful sign like that I was goin' to remember those words for the rest of my days."

Hannah died a few weeks later. She'd had a massive stroke while sleeping—no pain or suffering. I attended her funeral and paid my respects. Hundreds of people were there from all walks of life: lawyers, doctors, policemen—even a clown in a costume covered in bows and obnoxiously large buttons and tulips.

Her youngest son was seventy-four and gave her eulogy. It seemed that Hannah had really taken those words of Mr. Lincoln's seriously. She had been a modest woman, known by everyone for her kindness and volunteer work. Her son remembered her pecan pie and her keen sense of humor.

For years Hannah had held reading classes at her church for anyone of any color who could not read and her classes were well attended.

She and her former student, the clown, went to local hospitals and read to sick children.

Hannah was also heavily involved with the Civil Rights movement in the southern states. That came as no surprise to me. Her son remembered his mama going south nearly every school break where she taught older African-American people how to read and write so they would be able to vote. He was glad Hannah had lived long enough to see that day arrive.

I was a student nurse when I took care of Hannah, but I have never forgotten her. Though I did not develop vitiligo, I, too, have remembered Mr. Lincoln's words and have passed them on to many people, including my own children.

And every now and then an image flashes before me—Hannah and Abraham Lincoln having tea together, sharing cookies, the vanilla ones with strawberry jam centers, and smiling.

The Classic Question

Linda Aukett

Four years ago, my husband, Ken, was in the hospital for a bilateral knee replacement. Recognizing his gift for narrative, the medical staff asked if he would be a guinea pig for medical students early in their rotation, as they learned how to take a medical history. Having little else to do while the passive-motion machine exercised his healing legs, he gladly agreed.

He has a good medical story to tell about his long years with ulcerative colitis and the related arthritic condition that gradually wore out his knees. He can also keep a straight face when he needs to, and it came in handy as the students stopped in one by one, went through the history collection, and finally got around to the classic question, "When was your last bowel movement?" His answer, "1972," was an attention-grabber for each student, and he would take advantage of their full attention to tell them the advantages of having had an ileostomy that year. This particular class of students will be bound to remember the lesson he had to share about the quality of life that can be had without a colon.

Skaterboy
Ellen Javernick

Matt was our skaterboy; it wasn't surprising that he grew up to be an orthopedic surgeon. He'd smashed many a body part on the half pipe he'd built in our backyard. With his share of scans and scopes, he almost wasn't accepted into the army because an X-ray revealed that one of his crashes had caused a cracked pelvis.

Matt joined the army so he could attend USUHS (Uniformed Services University of the Health Sciences) Medical School in Washington, D.C. There, men and women from all branches of the service receive a free education in return for a commitment of seven years in the military after their residencies.

The regimes of medical school, internship, and residency were grueling even with new rules that discouraged hospitals from assigning young doctors to work more than eighty hours per week. Matt hated having to spend so much time away from his wife and baby.

When I moved back east to be their Granny Nanny, I noticed how tired and discouraged he seemed. I listened to his stories of young soldiers brought back from Iraq and Afghanistan to Walter Reed Medical Center where he worked. The plight of these young people rarely made the papers. For every death reported so prominently, five or six young men and women were injured, their lives irrevocably changed.

Matt explained that the horrible war wounds were first treated in the field, grit and shrapnel removed, emergency amputations performed, and patients stabilized. Then the injured were put on planes and transported to places like Walter Reed. Three times a week new casualties arrived with wounds to be washed and watched for infection, and arms and legs to be evaluated for additional amputation. Every day Matt had to share sad news with soldiers and their families. He had to tell his patients they'd never play soccer, or skateboard, or perhaps even walk again.

I prayed out loud for some way to transport Matt away from the suffering he had to witness on a daily basis. "If only I could win millions of dollars in the lottery, I'd repay the cost of your medical school and buy your way out of the army," I told him. Matt grinned, and then turned serious. "But, Mom, somebody has to take care of those kids. I think God deploys us to the places our talents are most needed." Maybe my skaterboy was in the right place after all.

The Message
Darlene Roy-Johnson

I was over fifty and my doctor advised me to get a colonoscopy. I scheduled the appointment and received the preparation instructions to clean out my colon. As I was completing the preparation, I had a silly idea. Since everyone's butt is the same, I decided to make mine stand out from the pack. Therefore, I gave my husband a black marker and asked him to write on the left cheek of my butt "Start Here" and draw an arrow pointing to my "Entrance." We chuckled about it all the way to the clinic.

When I arrived at the clinic, I was asked to put on a gown for the procedure. Even though the gown opened up in the back, I made sure no one saw my butt because I did not want to spoil the surprise. When it was time for my colonoscopy, I was lying on the table; the doctor opened up my gown and saw the message. She laughed out loud and reread it a couple of times, which made me laugh. Then she called in her assistants to view my special message and they laughed too.

I've Fallen and I Can't Get up!
Shirley Stille

Working as a registered nurse (RN) administrator in a rural county public health/homecare agency, I received an urgent call at 8:00 a.m. An aide and nurse could not get into a patient's home; they had looked in the windows per protocol and couldn't see him anywhere. With concern that the patient may have died or fallen, they called me and the patient's family member contact who met us at the home.

As the door was unlocked and we entered, we heard muffled noises coming from the bedroom. Once we got to the bedroom door, we saw a twin sized mattress on the floor wiggling about and two hands on each side moving, along with two feet at the far end wiggling. The family member started to laugh out loud and said, "My God, it's like a turtle that fell on his back and can't get turned over!"

Of course we saw the likeness and had a difficult time remaining professional. We got the patient out from under the mattress and sat him in a chair. He had fallen on his way back from the bathroom sometime during the night and crawled to the bed. Pulling on the bed to crawl in, he accidentally pulled the mattress off and on to himself.

Meanwhile, the family member can't get over the vision of the turtle on its back and can't stop laughing while he tells the poor patient what he looks like. Realizing he was okay except for a few rug burns and bruised ego, the patient also began to laugh and we laughed along with him.

The Medicine of Hope
Dennis Douda

The eleven-year-old boy was curled in a fetal position facing the wall, all the better to separate and define the vertebrae along the skinny child's spine. Such a cute kid. You could easily picture him romping through a Disney movie with a bunch of laughing, scrappy co-stars. He had dark red hair and freckles. A huge smile swept across his face as he recited pitching stats and batting averages for his heroic Minnesota Twins baseball team.

But, then the "tap team" arrived. The boy obediently lay down on his side and drew his knees up to his chest. Even though the procedure room at this highly regarded St. Paul children's hospital was warm, he trembled.

"How are you doing, Kelly?" The spinal tap technician called out as she rubbed the child's back and nodded sympathetically at Kelly's mother who was stroking her son's hair. "Okay," Kelly said bravely, even though his wavering voice betrayed a few doubts about how this would all turn out. Kelly had been diagnosed with leukemia.

A hissing noise grew louder at the head of Kelly's table. A nitrous oxide tank had been quietly wheeled into the room. "We have a little smiley gas for you, Kelly," said a friendly male nurse with spiked-up hair. The nurse placed a mask on the boy's face. "Regular, steady breaths, Bud." So-called "laughing gas" has been safely used for over a hundred years. Recently, this hospital found it to be a marvelous tool for dozens of highly stressful procedures its young patients must endure. Within ninety seconds, Kelly's taut frame visibly relaxed.

I'm a medical reporter and I had been so engrossed with the process of administering the laughing gas that, when I turned to see how the nurse specialist was progressing with the spinal tap, I felt my face flush fiery hot. Tears welled up in my eyes as I watched the tip of the needle pierce directly into Kelly's spinal column. More accurately, the target the needle found was a fluid-filled void around the delicate nerves that are critical for sending signals back and forth between Kelly's limbs and his brain. The nurse knows she is perfectly in position because the back of the needle is now dripping clear spinal fluid into a collection vial for testing.

For a moment I am in awe of the skilled hands of this young woman who so smoothly guided the needle. Then the feeling of awe turns to awful. A dark realization is dawning. To be become so skilled and efficient, the nurse has had a lot of practice. Too much practice. There have been too many Kellys lying on tables like these. I can easily picture the face of one of my sons lying there. I feel for every parent who has had a child lying on a table like this one.

I have been a medical reporter for CBS-owned WCCO-TV in Minnesota's Twin Cities for about ten years. Witnessing hundreds of surgeries has been one of the most educational parts of my job. Even watching eye surgery or an exposed brain pulsing with each beat of the heart is not enough to rattle me. But put a child in a life or death struggle and the steely, objective resolve of this reporter turns to jelly.

Fortunately, I know that never before could Kelly have had such fabulous tools of medicine at the disposal of his medical team. There is imaging equipment that allows doctors to examine the specifics of the cancer cells they are fighting. There are advanced cancer fighting medicines. New tests save doctors precious time by telling them early in the treatment process whether their chosen therapies are working or should be abandoned for other options. Among all the specialty fields of journalism that exist, I firmly believe I have been blessed with the absolute best news beat. Medical reporting truly is the journalism of hope.

In general, much of what the public gets from the news is tragic. Fires burn homes. Car wrecks take lives. Wars tear countries and civilizations and families apart. Sure, there are beats focused on the economy, education, politics, the environment, or society and they all involve reporting on honorable people trying to make the world a better place.

But writing about medicine allows one to tell the public about promising new research or medical breakthroughs that can make millions of lives better. And while citing the statistics of increased survivability of disease for the population at large, I also get to look into the eyes of a patient like Kelly and know the difference scientific advances make for a freckle-faced boy. Medical reporting is about finding the experts who are creating healthier lives for the masses, and delivering their gifts to one human being at a time.

With each new day come new discoveries, better ways to see, treat, and beat cancers of all kinds. Better ways to manage the nausea and the pain and the side effects of waging an ever more hopeful battle against The Big C. That was what my grandfather used to call cancer.

He told me once about a farmer friend of his down the road who got The Big C, as if even saying the word cancer out loud would beckon the plague of this mysterious, unspeakable disease to his household. Today, fortunately, cancer is a lot less mysterious.

For Kelly, that means greater understanding for what he is going through to get well and a lot more hope he will be memorizing Twins' stats for a lifetime of seasons to come.

Obadiah and Bernice

By Sterling Haynes

It was a sad day for me when I read in the *Toronto Globe & Mail* newspaper of the death of Coretta Scott King. As a doctor, I treated her aging parents for ten years.

In 1980, the U.S. Army and the U.S. Health Development Corporation recruited me to look after the medical needs of the people of Perry County and the cadets of Marion Military Institute. We left B.C. and we moved to Alabama where I practiced medicine and my wife, Jessie, ran the clinic.

Coretta Scott King was raised in Heiberger, Alabama, [a hamlet close to Marion] by her parents, Obadiah and Bernice Scott. Coretta was sent to a private missionary school and graduated first in her class at the Lincoln School in downtown Marion. Two patients in the new clinic were Obadiah and Bernice. They were well spoken, and as leaders of the black community, endorsed me as their doctor and spread the word that I was an "OK Doc." They gave me Coretta's phone number in Atlanta, and I was instructed to call Mrs. King, their daughter, if either of them developed major health problems. As Obie and Bernice were both in their eighties, I was phoning Atlanta quite regularly. Mrs. Coretta Scott King always had time to talk to me about her folks and Marion. I knew she was busy and was lobbying in Washington [in 1983] to have the third Monday of every January set aside as a national holiday—Martin Luther King Day.

Coretta Scott King was labeled by the press as cold and, at times, calculating. I never found that to be true. Whenever I phoned Atlanta, her voice was soft and slow. She was always focused and concerned. When her mother, Bernice, developed a malignancy, Mrs. Scott was moved. Mrs. Coretta Scott King arranged, the next day, for her mother to be transported to Emory's University Hospital in Atlanta for treatment.

Obie and Bernice were my regulars and only came when they had a serious medical problem. Obie was a small, sinewy, tough old man who still ran a small "Gro" in Heiberger. He was honest and wouldn't put up with any nonsense. He packed a .44 revolver under the counter of his grocery store, so he said, and practiced with the gun every dawn, shooting at targets.

Nobody messed with Obie. He would always phone for an appointment for nine o'clock and was always with Bernice. He would get very impatient if he wasn't seen immediately and sometimes would pitch a fit if there was a delay. He demanded to be seen first until one day in my office, Bernice hit Obie with her purse and demanded that *she* be seen first.

"Obie, you're always barging in ahead of me and speaking for me. I can speak for myself and you get out of here until I talk to the doctor." After this episode, Bernice always seemed to be in charge.

Bernice, at eighty-five years, was still a tall beautiful woman. Eloquent in her speech but still as feisty as Obie. We became good friends, but I always saw her first in the morning despite Obie's scowls.

The Scotts always applauded me for having the first non-segregated medical clinic in Marion, open to all. Everyone, black or white, was free to use our flush toilets and to drink ice water from our water fountains. During the summer heat, all fifty waiting room chairs were in use—everyone enjoyed the air-conditioned waiting room and the daily gossip. Obie was a local African-American leader and he always knew when I'd made house calls in the black section of Marion.

Obie and Bernice were very proud of their middle daughter, Coretta, and Martin, their son-in-law. They were a special pair, and I often think of that memorable speech Martin Luther King gave to over two hundred thousand people at the Lincoln Memorial Center in Washington in 1963. It exemplified the philosophy of all the Scotts.

When I decided to retire from medicine and return to British Columbia, Obie brought us watermelons galore and Bernice baked us a pound cake. Bernice hugged my neck and Obie, age ninety-two, shook my hand and told me I was one of the first "whitey's" that he ever trusted.

Confessions of a Candy Striper
Eileen Mitchell

When I was sixteen, I was a volunteer candy striper for a local hospital, possibly the worst volunteer of all time, shattering the myth that a warm body is better than no body at all. My contribution to humanity could have been considered detrimental.

As a clueless teenager, my work at the hospital was more like a blooper reel than a resume builder. I did everything wrong, I walked in on people in various states of undress (curiously, men didn't seem to mind, but the women sure did), and I tried to deliver flowers to someone receiving last rites. I asked new mothers in the maternity ward when they were expecting their babies unaware that post-partum weight loss takes time. I told a fellow candy striper to inform visitors that the patient they were looking for had checked out because it said "expired" on his information card. The patient checked out—not only out of the hospital, but out of this world!

I delivered a patient to the wrong wing of the hospital, and I took a patient to the wrong floor perplexed at why the doors were locked only to learn later it was the psychiatric ward. I struggled, painfully slowly, to push a man twice my size in a wheelchair. He kept asking why it was taking so long, and when we finally reached the elevator, I discovered the brakes were on. At least I didn't injure anybody—other than myself. Let's face it, I don't think I was cut out for a career in the health care field, but I sure enjoyed prancing around in that cute pink-and-white striped pinafore.

Lost and Found

Carol McAdoo Rehme

My finger found the familiar button and pressed.

"Yes?" answered the faceless intercom.

"Mother here to see Kyle in bed eleven."

"Give us thirty minutes. X-ray is with him."

Another wait. My friend Vickie and I sat in the alcove near the staff elevator. Now accustomed to operating on hospital time and within hospital rules, we settled ourselves on the narrow seat. Silently, somberly. She read her book; I wrote in my journal.

We'd spent a lot of time waiting outside the trauma unit since my son had been admitted, the victim of a hit and run. Having a friend around lightened the load and my days. Although he was still comatose, Kyle was steadily improving and I was daring to hope. And to smile again.

Finally, one hour and thirty minutes later, we were allowed into the trauma unit. Standing at the sink in Kyle's cubicle, I massaged antiseptic suds between my fingers.

"Why was X-ray here?" I asked over my shoulder.

"They wanted to get films of Kyle's sinuses," answered the young resident doctor. "They suspect an infection."

"But I thought they did that yesterday."

"They couldn't find them."

Puzzled, I shook off the water droplets, dried my hands, and looked up. "They couldn't find them?"

"No," answered the doctor, "they lost them."

"They lost his sinuses?" I was stunned.

"No," he said with measured preciseness. "They lost his X-rays."

Vickie snickered. The doctor grinned. I blushed.

"Oh, I know all about that, I lose socks nearly every time I do laundry like there's some vast gaping hole they fall into and disappear forever, never to be seen again," I babbled on and on.

Vickie grinned. The doctor snickered. I snapped my mouth shut.

Two days later we warmed the alcove bench again, waiting on yet another series of X-rays.

"What is it this time?" I had asked.

"Sinus."

"But we've done that twice already! What happened?"

"They lost them," answered the same resident.

"They lost the X-rays?" My eyebrows shot up. I couldn't believe it.

"No," he winked, "this time they lost the sinuses!"

And they had. The second series of pictures had showed nothing. Clouded and foggy, the defective film was deemed worthless by the embarrassed staff.

The Surprise Nurse

Stephanie Devine

I was a normal, healthy stay-at-home mom of two vibrant young boys, and I had a part-time job playing piano and organ for my church. I loved hanging out with my husband, our many friends, and enjoyed riding horses and Jazzercising.

One day, I was stricken with a terrible flare up of Crohn's disease. I probably had the irritable bowel disease much of my life, but in typical busy-mom style, ignored the symptoms that had been manageable until now. At 2:00 in the morning I was rushed by ambulance to the hospital with excruciating abdominal pain. It felt as if I was giving birth to a baby—sideways.

A week later in the hospital, my bowel perforated; emergency surgery left me with a temporary ileostomy. The roller coaster of emotions and physical pain was a shock coming from a life of relative normality. I was completely incapacitated and dealing with a piece of my small intestine dangling on my belly to boot.

The hospitalization journey brought me an amazing cast of characters. Much like the diverse people encountered at the state fair, in a hospital there was a cavalcade of people who came in my room on a rotating basis. The nurses had the greatest impact on me. The majority were kind and compassionate, held my hand when I was down, rushed to my assistance when summoned, and dealt with my intravenous tubes without a hint of annoyance.

There was also the drill sergeant nurse, or as my husband affectionately called her, the "Kathy Bates from the scary Stephen King film nurse," along with a couple of nurses who seemed utterly dispassionate and clueless. My favorite nurse met me when I was newly operated on, soaking in a haze of drugs and pain. I smelled, and had tubes containing bodily fluids pouring forth from my body. When the 11:00 p.m. shift began, in walked one of the most handsome men who I swear must have stepped right out of a Chippendale's lineup. With a deep, sexy voice to match he said, "Hi, I'm your nurse for the evening. My name is Derek."

I assumed he was a candy gram sent by my hilarious friends, and I waited for the rose, the kiss, and a cheery "get well soon!" or maybe he was a mirage brought on by the drugs and would morph back into the Kathy Bates nurse. I soon realized that Derek was real, a very adept nurse who clearly lifted weights regularly as he hefted me from the bed as if I was a feather. Once it became obvious that Derek wasn't from my imagination, I noticed he provided a ray of sunshine in my dismal hospital experience. I'm thankful Derek passed up his modeling career in favor of attending to sick folks like me. Even though I never saw Derek again, he lives in my memory as a good nurse.

Pushing Pills
Paris Purnell

Sometimes night duty as a nurse can get a tad, shall we say—uninteresting. During the wee hours of the night, one's mind starts to turn to all sorts of things, and sometimes fatigue renders things in less than 20/20 vision with regards to clear thinking. I was still in my youth and had just gotten a new pair of roller blades that I was trying to master. I thought it would be good to get some practice in during the 6:00 a.m. medication round when everyone was starting to wake up.

Resembling a flight attendant serving beverages off a cart, the medication round is similar except the patient receives medication that really makes them feel better and can make a major difference in their day. I sailed in with the drug trolley on my roller blades while efficiently snapping on the lights. It raised a few eyebrows but got everyone awake while they watched amused as they witnessed an idiot wheeling a trolley while fighting gravity and crashing into walls.

Perhaps it wasn't a good idea at the time, but it was heartwarming to see patients almost laughing their insides out. Later, I loaned the roller blades to the other nurse on duty—a female who was much shorter and with tiny feet. She did a sterling job until she lost control and hit the fire exit door at the end of the corridor and promptly disappeared. At least she was in the right place if something untoward happened—thankfully she was okay, just a mess of giggling hysteria! So rest assured, while you are sleeping in your hospital room at night, the staff is not. They are often thinking of creative ways to help with the best medicine—laughter.

Motion Commotion
Pamela Gregg

Several years ago, I suffered some inner ear trouble that caused bouts of dizziness. We're not talking about a swaying room or lightheadedness here; it was a crippling, bring-you-to-your-knees, room-is-spinning-as-fast-as-a-CD-in-a-player dizziness. The ambulance came and the paramedics brought me out in a cot with wheels and loaded me into the rig, and we zipped off. At the first stop sign, however, when the driver hit the brakes to slow down, the wheel lock gave way and the cot broke free, sending me forward toward the cab with the drivers. Since I was already dizzy, the extra motion combined with the ensuing jolt when the cot bounced off a back wall brought my already twisted stomach into knots. The EMT (emergency medical technician) in the back of the rig with me yelled at the driver that he hadn't secured me properly. The driver screamed back that the wheel lock must have malfunctioned and instructed the EMT to pop the cot into the wheel lock with force. She grabbed the end of my flying cot, moved it several inches away from the lock, and tried to secure the lock by jerking it. The attempt failed just as we were rounding a corner and sent me on another joy ride.

I whimpered quietly while the rear EMT yelled again. The driver hit the brakes sending my trusty steed cot and me in yet another direction. The extra motion would have brought me to my knees if I hadn't already been lying down. To make matters worse, the rig's medicine kit was minus Phenergan, an antiemetic normally on board. The driver instructed the EMT to open the back doors of the rig and climb out in order to give herself some room to really swing the end of that cot. I kept thinking, *you've got to be kidding. This is too cruel to even be on a sitcom.* Standing on the street and bracing herself for the thrust, the EMT moved me a couple of feet to the right and then WHAM! I prayed as she tried to get the wheel to catch in the lock. *No luck.* My whimpering grew louder. One more time, BAM. *Still no good.* Moaning loudly in protest, the EMT met my childish vocalization with a scolding, "Oh, for Pete's sake, you're fine." With one last mighty thrust, she slammed the cot into the lock. *Success!* The EMT climbed aboard and we sped off without further incident. If I hadn't already had crippling motion sickness when I called them, I sure would have gotten it on my ambulance ride.

When I returned from the hospital, I called the local fire chief to tell him that he had a rig, an EMT, and a medicine kit that sorely needed attention. I might have to consider a taxi if it happens again!

Pat

Mark Kennedy

In our company, we teach and sell a bowel management system called Ac-tiFlo Indwelling Bowel Catheter. We often demonstrate the techniques used on a physiologically androgynous torso we refer to as PAT. As I had checked out of my room already, I had to clean up the reinforced anus of one of our "PATs" in the restroom of the Marriott Hotel adjacent to the hospital after giving an in-service for sixty nurses. In order to demonstrate proper insertion technique with PAT, it is necessary to lubricate the business end of the bowel management system liberally. In between demonstrations, however, it is essential to remove all remaining lubricant so that it does not harden into a rigid crust around the anus. Right as I literally had my hand up PAT's behind with a paper towel, two janitors barged into the public rest room and immediately yelled out, "Boy, what the f--- are you doing?"

Naturally, it took a good five minutes to explain to them what was going on. I'm still not quite sure they believed me.

Bedpan Bedlam

Brenda Elsagher

I had my knees operated on in the mid seventies and the care for knee recovery was entirely different from what it is now. These days you are up within hours practically running down the hall after surgery. You get a mechanism that makes your knee bend right out of surgery. Back then, you didn't get going right away. It was probably a couple of days before I got up to walk. And part of the building muscle strength process was lifting buckets of sand with my foot. That wouldn't happen today, the rehabilitation process is different as well.

The nurse brought a bedpan to me and explained I would use that until I could get into the bathroom. As a seventeen-year-old, that was just too odd and I couldn't go. I felt like I was under some kind of performance anxiety. The idea of another person looking at my bodily fluids really bothered me.

The nurse and my friends started giving me suggestions. Think of waterfalls. They turned on the water faucet to try to inspire me. Success finally happened while I lay on that big, cold, solid metal basin under my tush. Someone got me a bowl of warm water and I was instructed to put my hand in it. I did and Eureka! You'll enjoy the stories in this section even if they aren't all Eureka! moments.

The Orderly

Hump Elsen

The year was 1974, and I had to go to the hospital with disk problems from lifting improperly. I'd had previous aches and pains with my back, some that even required traction and medication before they got better, but it had been awhile. I felt fairly strong at that time and lifted tires regularly, so I didn't think much about it when I threw a semi truck wheel up over the side of my tow truck until I felt the surging pain in my back. Later that day I couldn't get straightened up.

I was referred to a chiropractor, and I went to see him. Up to that point I had only seen an orthopedic doctor. The chiropractor had a nice new modern low table and when I got on it, he cranked on my legs and told me I'd need some more treatments. By the time I got home, it was bad again. I went back later for another treatment, but when I went to get off the table, it was too low and the chiropractor and my wife had to help me off. Later they tried electric shock pads on the muscles to loosen them, but it only seemed to make things worse.

By the time I went to see my old orthopedic doctor, I couldn't even button my shirt because I couldn't put both of my feet flat on the ground without tremendous pain. He watched me shake as I buttoned my shirt and he said, "The time is up; we'll probably have to do the surgery in three different stages. You have to have disk repairs, and we'll need to clip the tips off of your vertebrae so they will line up straight. How are you doing with the drugs? Are you still able to sleep better?"

"Fine," I said. "I'm leaving for the horse races."

"That's okay as long as you don't drink with those, that's a potent mix."

"You should have told me that three years ago! No wonder I always had a lot of fun at the parties."

Surgery was scheduled soon after. My doctor suggested I go downtown, "They are better equipped to handle people of your size." I come from a family of tall and big people with my brothers and I standing well over six feet. I was the baby in the family but the biggest of all of them. While I was in the hospital awaiting surgery, a visiting nun in the Catholic hospital came to see me. She didn't know what I did for a living, but she said,

"In the old days, you never used to see farmers with as much back trouble because they were walking on soft ground. They didn't walk on black top or concrete."

That was her theory. She didn't know that at the time I was working nine to ten hours a day at a family service station, which was all concrete. I jumped off and on tow trucks all day long, and I drove a garbage truck part-time to support my eight children and wife.

Surgery was nearly six hours long and the doctors came out to talk to my wife, Helen.

"He must have been taking a lot of aspirin because his bones are so hard." The doctor was getting tired and he was concerned I was losing too much blood. "I have to sew him back up and quit for now."

I was told I had to remain still and not move in recovery. I had so many muscle spasms that I was all over the bed because they had been tightened up for so long. I was in the hospital for ten days, went home for three weeks, and then had to go back in to the hospital for four more hours of surgery so he could finish up. They pumped a lot of morphine into me. One night I woke up sweating and cold. They changed my sheets several times. I felt slimy. Later I told a nurse, "I think I'm a Vaseline bottle."

"No, you're withdrawing from the drugs," she answered.

I lay like a log after the second surgery. They had a pillow between my legs, and I was instructed to roll like a log and not separate my legs.

The main attendant I had was an orderly that was also a big guy. He used to tease me and I gave it back to him. I had an elderly man for a roommate that had hip surgery and he had a lot of visitors. I told him if he had company when I had to pass wind, I was going to have to let it go. I tried to hold it off at first, and then I just couldn't anymore and I felt a little better.

After several days, I hadn't eaten anything but Jell-O, and they decided I had to have an enema after visiting hours. They gave me the enema and put me on a bedpan. I woke up about three in the morning and asked them to remove that bedpan. I felt like I had a metal washer (like the kind they put around a bolt) bolted around my butt.

Later that morning, I finally had the feeling that the enema was taking affect. My orderly friend came on at 7:00 a.m. Embarrassed about myself, I teased him, "I've been waiting for you, and I've got a special gift for you."

He was not happy about the clean up job that was necessary. He pulled the sheets off one half at a time. He rolled me over halfway on the bed and along the way my hand knocked the water glass off the table and onto the floor. After he finished cleaning that side, he went to roll me over to clean the other side when my hand caught the water pitcher and it went all over the floor. After he had it all cleaned up, we were bantering back and forth and the orderly said, "You think you're funny, Big Guy?" He laughed as he gave me a spanking!

Things Go Better With Coke
Brenda Kuhlman

In 1976, patients remained in the hospital at least ten days post-op. In my case, it was longer. But I was young, impatient, and feeling stronger, thanks to my new ileostomy. I was ready to resume my life. I asked visiting friends to bring me something I'd been denied for a long time—soda. I didn't care that it could cause gas. My friends must have returned while I was napping, because I awoke to find two cans of Coke resting in an ice-filled bedpan.

I raised my can of soda in a silent tribute to life's tiny pleasures, and drank heartily. Then I went back to sleep.

The next day my doctor appeared, a worried expression on his face. He ordered my nurse to put in an IV drip. When I asked why, he said he was concerned about dehydration. Seems the measured urine output for the previous day was abnormally high.

It wasn't until the following day that I realized my nurse had measured the melted ice cubes in the bedpan!

Bedpan Basics
Paris Purnell

I don't know why, but working as a nurse you can sometimes see the humor in bedpans. When requested by two women at once in the same room, I would often get the two and bang them together like a cheerleader—down, left, right, and up over my head. It seemed to take the edge off a male nurse helping women when it could be embarrassing!

There is a stool test for microbiology that requires the specimen to be delivered hot to the laboratory. I derived great satisfaction running through the department yelling, "Hot stool—hot stool," like a hot dog seller—much to the chagrin of my charge nurse.

Attending a friend's twenty-first party—also a nurse—he had a new bedpan and filled it with French onion dip and crackers. Quite the talking point if you want to liven up a dull party.

The Sarcastic Nurse
LaDonna Joseph

In 1970, in nursing school, I hurriedly placed an empty, metal bedpan on the edge of the bed. My teacher and I went to reposition the patient; the bedpan fell off the bed making a very loud sound. The teacher looked at me with a deadpan expression, "Bedpan's are *not glued* to the bed."

CHAPTER 6

Just for Jollies

Brenda Elsagher

Even a hospital room setting has potential for a good time. My dear friend Sherry was recovering from surgery after dealing with a serious attack of diverticulitis. I was on my way to visit her in the hospital and called Sherry from my cell phone to let her know when I would arrive.

"Hi, Sherry, how are you feeling today?" I asked.

"Brenda, both Jen and Kris are here, Doug is here, and our daughters brought us cards and flowers because it's our forty-fourth wedding anniversary."

"Sounds like you have enough company for now, I'll come another time," I said, even though I was only five minutes away. I turned my car off at the next exit and went to the nearby liquor store and bought two bottles of champagne and some plastic champagne glasses, the really deluxe kind of glasses where you twist the stem into the bottom piece. The cashier put the bottles in pretty bags, put bows on them, and off I went to the hospital to surprise Sherry and Doug.

I walked into the room and with delight in her voice to see me, Sherry was glad I had lied. Her daughters, Jenny and Kris, were sitting nearby; Doug, her husband, stood close and Sherry seemed happy to be surrounded by all the love in the room. I announced it was time to celebrate their anniversary with champagne. Doug laughed as I handed him the bottles and they giggled when I brought out the champagne flutes. After the quick assembling, we poured champagne all around and toasted the happy couple.

"Can I drink some of this?" Sherry asked the nurse who popped in to check her vitals just then.

"I don't think a sip will hurt you, go ahead," she said with a smile.

We emptied a bottle in no time and talked further about that afternoon. The nurse walked back in.

"I've worked here twelve years, and I've never seen anyone bring champagne in before," she said.

"Well, I was thinking about that on the way over here," I said. "Then I figured this is a Catholic hospital, Jesus was the first person we ever heard about turning water into wine at the wedding at Cana, this is my friends' anniversary, and the Catholics love Jesus, so it seemed like the right thing to do."

"Can't argue with that logic," she said laughing and walked out the door. It was a great celebration in an unusual setting, I saw Sherry relax for the first time in quite a while, which made it all the better. Cheers to the happy couple!

There are many memorable moments that happen because of medical issues and the following stories reveal the hope, humor, and optimism that often accompany them. Cheers!

Senior Ladies Swim
Barbara Jay Nies

In the locker room and pool, there thrives a special camaraderie among we aged, ailing, handicapped, specially-abled, and misshapen gathered for Senior Ladies Swim from 2:00 to 3:00 in the afternoon. We laugh and reminisce and exchange recipes and war stories, and we even swim. But there must be something in the water because...

We ignore that some of our high cheekbones have morphed into jowls and our jowls have become wattles. We pay no attention to the facts that once voluptuous and luscious breasts and arms and thighs have withdrawn from their skin slings and have migrated south to insulate and hide waistlines and the high hip pads (ambitiously still called love handles) and even kneecaps. Some of us have even grown our own aprons–lucky ducks! And almost all our collective biceps skin flaps freely in the breeze.

Even though our hair sadly misrepresents itself in its crowning glory days, we treat it as tenderly as we can afford, carefully cap it against the chlorinated water of the pool, and compliment each other generously on its cut and curl and the glamour of the swimcap. We use lotions and potions as expensive as our purses and hope can afford, and reassure each other that our skin is not mottled, mutilated, splotched, scarred, glottled, stopped, sagging, bagging, lagging, and tired.

We compliment each other on the cut of new swimsuits, and old ones, since we can no longer compliment each other on the cut of our jibs. We mutually agree that we all still have "figures" and not "builds." We have professional manicures and pedicures of nails, more often than not, discolored, ridged, chipped, or fungicacious, to coin a phrase, and once more feel "pretty, oh so pretty. pretty, witty, and gay," etc. at Senior Ladies Swim.

By mutual consent, we don't notice that many of our buttocks no longer retain the hormonal fullness and muscularity of youth and young matronage; that many have shrunken to lean, angular lobes that don't begin to fill the seats of swimsuits and slacks, for instance–unless they have burgeoned beyond all Weight Watchers' worst nightmares and our cups do indeed runneth over–over the top, down the sides, and sometimes pooling around ankles and feet.

We ignore the wens, warts, liver spots, and barnacles that impart so much character to our arms, faces, and private places. We never note that our hairy spots have gone bald while four-inch Hobbit tufts of white bristles sprong overnight through our skin at stunning places. Although our glasses are strong, our hearing aids weak, and our teeth stained, we are very kind and loving to our sisterhood of the swim.

…but less so, sadly, to our own selves, when we look into the mirrors of the world outside the pool and locker room at Senior Ladies' Swim. Must indeed be something in the water.

Saving Soles
Dorothy Rosby

When a medical professional says, "You need surgery," many thoughts race through your mind, the main one being, "Isn't there an easier way to get some time off?"

In my case, the nurse even showed me a matter-of-fact video about the procedure the doctor was recommending. I think this was meant to make my upcoming double bunionectomy seem as easy as having my tires rotated. Still, I left the doctor's office in a daze, tormented by all the questions I *wished* I'd asked. And to make matters worse, someone called the day before the surgery to ask me a long list of questions, including whether I have advanced directives and a living will. I said, "Wait a minute! I'm having foot surgery."

"This is just to be on the safe side."

"Whose safe side?"

This conversation did nothing to help me sleep that night. And I thought *I should sleep.* Then I thought, *Why? I'm not the one doing the work tomorrow.*

I reported to the surgery center the next morning very tired and with nothing but the clothes on my back—and not even my best ones. As you know, women are instructed not to wear jewelry or make-up on surgery day. And to be fair, I don't think men should either.

Women have been told not to bring a purse. And as any woman will tell you, being without your purse is like being naked. In short order, you're that way too. Of course, I was given a gown (warmer than the paper ones you wear in a clinic, but not as attractive).

I was led into a large room filled with busy medical professionals dressed in colorful clothing. And I remember thinking, *How nice that they all wear colors now instead of white like they did long ago. It's so much more cheerful. And color won't show the blood as badly.* And then I remember thinking, *I wish I didn't think so much.*

A very nice man, wearing what looked like pajamas, told me he was going to give me something to help me relax. Then I quit thinking altogether. Eventually, I woke up feeling like I wanted to sleep—very similar to the way I feel on Monday mornings. Nurses came and went. I didn't care. They did things to me. I didn't care. When the anesthesia wore off, they sent me home with a lovely pair of surgical shoes. One size doesn't quite fit all—but one shoe does fit either foot.

Then came recovery. The flowers and painkillers, the attention and time off were all very nice, but I think it would have been less expensive and more interesting to take a cruise. I wasn't even fully recovered when the bills started arriving. There were bills from the surgery clinic, the doctor, the anesthesiologist, the lab, and the manufacturer of the surgical shoes.

For once, something exceeded credit card offers in my mailbox. This did nothing to aid in my recovery. Not only could I not pay all the bills, I couldn't understand them. Medical bills are the reason so many people have life-saving procedures, then go ahead and die anyway.

Recovery wasn't all bad, though. I spent a month with my feet up, reading, playing solitaire, and ordering my husband around—which normally I would *never* do.

I soon learned that daytime television is perfect for sick people and people under the influence of painkillers, because apparently it's created by sick people—sick, sick people—and people under the influence—of something.

I learned that playing army with my son, a game I've not always enjoyed, is more enjoyable when I get to lie on the couch and pretend to be a wounded soldier.

And I learned how gratifying it is to say, "Honey, *While, you're up*, could you . . ." My husband has often used that on me and now I know why. *While you're up*, could you get me a cup of tea? *While you're up*, could you turn up the heat? *While you're up*, could you paint the house?

This was so pleasant that I started to envision a very long recovery. I pictured myself welcoming visitors from my place on the couch, and saying pitifully, "Please forgive me if I don't get up; I just had surgery."

They would say, "I'm sorry! When?" and I would answer, "Nine years ago. Could you hand me that cheese dip—*while you're up?*"

Rollin' Along
Bahgat Elsagher

My brother was getting rehabilitation in a nursing home while recovering from surgery. He had a roommate that was a retired pilot with a terrible attitude. He always seemed to have a bad day and it appeared that whenever he would need to use the bathroom, it would be occupied or being cleaned. In his frustration, he decided to go down the hall to use the main bathroom on the floor for the use of the general public.

Within a few minutes he was back with his usual litany of complaints. Unbeknownst to him, he was dragging the roll of toilet paper all the way down the hall and it was stuck to his rear end.

My brother turned to me and said, "What is that?"

I told him, "I think he's getting a fax!" and we both laughed heartily.

Laryngitis Teaches Painful Lesson

Dorothy Rosby

You just don't know how much you talk until you can't do it anymore. You're probably thinking, "Speak for yourself." And that's exactly what I'm doing. I'm speaking for myself again, *finally,* after three days of not being able to speak for me or anybody else.

Like all other body parts, we completely take our vocal cords for granted until they aren't working properly. And mine didn't work *at all* for three *long* days. It was very nearly torture to me, though it must have been a pleasant respite to those around me. When I opened my mouth to speak, only a hoarse whisper came out. I was the "hoarse whisperer," and I don't see how it would make a good movie.

At work, I kept to my office, avoiding the breakroom, normally my favorite spot. I sat staring at my ringing telephone rather than pick it up and whisper into it. Maybe I'm old fashioned, but I believe that if you're going to whisper on the telephone, you should be the one placing the call.

At home I relied on my son to answer the phone, though I was concerned he'd sign us up for a new phone service and a stack of credit cards. He had bigger worries. On my first full day of silence, he asked, "How are you going to call us for supper?"

The little sign language I know was not helpful. I can make the sign for "thank you" which seems useful, and "I love pizza" which does not, though "get me a pizza" might be. Of course, it's possible that when I *think* I'm gesturing "thank you" or "I love pizza," I'm actually saying, "There's something in your teeth" and "What have you done to your hair?" Besides, sign language would only be helpful if everyone around me could understand it. Even then, one can only accomplish so much repeating "I love pizza" and even less with "There's something in your teeth."

The most painful part of my forced silence was the realization that I talk a lot more than I realize and, even worse, a great deal of what I say would be better left unsaid. Each time I was tempted to speak during those three long days, which was often, I had to weigh the importance of what I wanted to say against the pain and effort of forcing a whisper. Most of the time, it wasn't worth it. I wanted to yell at my son for misplacing his shoe—again. I'm glad I didn't; I had misplaced mine too. I wanted to tell the man in front of me at the grocery store that he had more than thirteen items, which was true. Then I realized I had fourteen. I wanted to scream at a truckload of teenagers that nearly ran me over. Just as well I didn't. They may have turned around and finished the job.

The experience led me to vow to weigh my words more carefully once my voice returned. I would become a woman of few, well-chosen words. And then, in the middle of my fourth silent night, I stepped on a small toy in the dark and swore out loud—few words, but not well chosen. That's when I realized my voice was back. It sounded like a Canadian honker, but it was back.

Of course, with my first words in three days being swear words, I had already failed in my pledge. That was almost as sobering as realizing that the most important thing I say all day is, "Supper is ready."

Healthy Friendships
Sari Jo Legge

With my vast experience of gastrointestinal issues, my healthy friends rely on me to guide them through medical procedures whenever they need any butts and guts medical care. One of my friends was having GERD (gastro esophageal reflux disease) and IBS (irritable bowel syndrome) issues, so her GI (gastroenterologist) scheduled her for a day of upper and lower scoping. She was to be blissfully knocked out for this. I was her designated driver and hand holder. On the day of the test, having changed into her hospital gown, we sat together until it was time to get her IV started.

She had minimal stage fright for a "scope novice," and her bowel prep the night before had been successful.

While waiting, she turned to me and asked, "Is there anything further I should know?"

I turned to her, looked her in the eye, and earnestly replied, "Don't worry; they do the esophageal test first before they put the hose in the other end. Sometimes they get mixed up, but that's unusual."

My Leg is a Frozen Rolled Roast
Janie Jasin

Preparation for replacement knee surgery came in the form of a class held at the hospital a week before the actual operation. Nurse Belinda ran through the details as she held a chart showing a face going from smiling to grimacing and asking what number on a scale of 1-10 accompanied the face. This chart and its numbering system would help the patient and nurses keep us ahead of the pain using our medications.

"Never wait until the pain is upon you," said Belinda, the RN.

This should have been a big warning to me, *PAIN*. I listened and when the class ended, we all marched down to the physical therapy department where a cute, professional woman measured me. She asked, "Does this hurt? That hurt? How about this? How far can you move this?"

I said, "It only hurts when I bend the knee. That is why I am having the surgery!" She finished measuring me and waved me off.

Soon, it was admitting day. Dropped off by my administrative assistant complete with rolling suitcase, I headed up to the third floor. Stripped, unpacked, and after several more blood lettings, I was ready for the trip to surgery. Wearing a bare outfit, no undies, and a shower cap on my head, I was rolled into surgery with people tending to me. It seemed they were doing some redecorating or remodeling. Someone was hanging drapes with a click, click, and a click. Then the green drape was lowered, and at the end of my surgical table was a man wrapping some sort of prosthesis. *Mmmm?* I thought. *Looks like a leg ready for a very tall person.* The surgeon's assistant was wrapping this long, headless, artificial leg well. I smiled and acknowledged his presence. It never registered that this was *my* leg he was wrapping. The sound earlier, similar to drapes being hung, was staples being put into my leg.

Wheeled from surgery to recovery, the class motto of "Keep ahead of your pain" went out the window. I was definitely behind it, and I was puffing, screeching, and writhing through it. The nurses and assistants came running with ice packs, meds for my arm and under my tongue, and a tube in every orifice. The health professionals seemed eager to move me this way and that, totally oblivious that this was my slalom leg, showing off arabesque leg, dancing leg, aerobic teacher leg. It was my best leg, now turned into a frozen rolled roast.

The next day, I was taken down to rehab, where Joan and I began our relationship.

"Lift the frozen roast," said Joan. "Bend the roast, slide the roast, measure the bend, stretch like a hurdler, stretch your hamstrings. Mmmmm! See you tomorrow!"

As I graduated from rehab roast school, my leg still had a few numb or frozen parts, the scar needed massage, the joint was a bit stiff, the progress slow but steady. My health care team all worked at the thawing and flexibility possibilities. They made me feel like a champion and an athlete while doing simple little bendy but tough things. I looked at this sixty-three-year-old leg that I often took for granted; I scanned the cellulite and what I thought was a lack of beauty. I promised to myself never to put my leg of wonder down again. This leg of mine is a healer, a strong pillar of power taking new steps. I looked at my medical center with new respect, admiration, and gratitude and knew the nurses were angels and wizards.

The physical therapists were tireless cheerleaders who calmed my soul and encouraged my most feeble attempts. My surgeon made it happen, and his assistant wrapped it up. My final appointment came just as the movie *Chicago* came out. As the surgeon asked me how it was going, I leapt up and sang as I danced.

"I'm going to rouge my knees and roll my stockings down. And "ALL THAT JAZZ."

He said, "I never had a patient dance at her last appointment."

My frozen roast had thawed into a dancing leg.

CHAPTER 7

Bowels Gone Berserk

Brenda Elsagher

When I was first facing the physical and emotional changes of dealing with colorectal cancer, I went to a support group in Minneapolis at a place called Pathways, a health crisis center for people with chronic illness or life threatening diseases.

I took an eight-week class that met once a week and started on time at 10:00 in the morning whether you were there or not. We had been told to be respectful of others by avoiding being late. It was a big deal to miss a class, and I had to be conscious of the time and plan ahead daycare for my two small children at home before getting myself ready, which involved spending time making sure my new colostomy pouch was secure and that I was prepared with extra supplies.

In those early days of learning about my colostomy, I had a lot of physical challenges getting my pouch to stay on or even seal properly. It seemed I was always running behind. Since the class was forty minutes away from my house, I had to be more conscious of the extra time it would take to get there. Mornings always seemed to be rushed as I prepared to leave the house.

One morning before class, it was time to change my pouch after showering. I realized in the middle of the process that I had left a component in my bedroom drawer. As I quickly stepped from the bathroom to my bedroom to grab it, planning to lunge back to the bathroom within three seconds, poop flew from my abdomen all over my bed, my carpet, and into the bathroom. I was already on a time crunch, and I began to cry. Besides, the whole experience was weird and gross.

I was wailing into my pity party out of frustration and anger, adjustment blues, and horror at the thought of dealing with this the rest of my life. I seemed to compose myself enough and knew I would be late. I had no choice, I couldn't leave my poop all over and cleaning that mess would take time. I called Pathways to let them know I would be delayed.

There was a ritual at the beginning of each of the meetings at Pathways called "Brags and Bummers" from the Renewing Life program offered there. We would each say something positive (brag) and a negative (bummer) we had encountered since we last saw each other. That exercise took some time to do but it was always good to hear about everyone else. When I finally arrived, I walked in at the moment when the last person was saying their brag and bummer.

I shared mine and explained they were one in the same. The bummer and reason I was late was because poop went flying out at an inopportune moment in my bedroom and bathroom and it required my immediate attention. The brag was instead of carrying on all day in my pity party for one, I got to work cleaning up myself and my room, stopped crying, and then put on the prettiest dress I owned, a bright blue and purple outfit, and went out into the world to face the day as a person living with an ostomy. We all have our bad moments, but they usually pass. It's how we handle them that counts. The stories in this section remind us of that.

A Good Life

Claribel Hawkins

In 1954, I became very sick and was in and out of the hospital for two years before I was diagnosed with ulcerative colitis. The doctors tried all sorts of medications, hoping they would prevent surgery. The colitis was caused by a microscopic organism and one medication I used was arsenic. I would mix a small amount with water and drink it halfway through my meals. Several times a small amount dropped on the porcelain sink and it turned the spot snow white; it was very strong.

With my illness accelerating, I weighed only eighty-six pounds at age thirty-three and I was scared; surgery was the only answer. The doctors took my entire colon, and I stayed in the hospital for eleven days with surgery costs of almost $300.00. This was a lot of money for my husband, Martin, and me. Our neighbors took up a collection and brought it to the hospital in a brown paper bag. On the outside of the bag was a list of the people that had given and the amount; some gave ten cents, others fifty cents, and several gave a dollar. People gave what they could, and their love for us was worth millions.

With my first surgery, there were problems with my ileostomy and the stoma [the end of the intestine that protrudes through the abdomen to discharge bodily waste] stuck out about three inches, requiring a skin graft from my leg to graft onto the stoma. The first appliance I used by Hollister had a white pad I put on around the stoma, then a bag that was attached with belts. To empty the bag, I had to take the appliance completely off each time. It didn't fit snugly like the one I use today. I have had several reconstructive surgeries and now the stoma is much smaller and the appliances much better. I was fortunate to have been married to Martin for sixty-one years before he died in 2002. I am eighty-five years old and have lived with an ileostomy for fifty-two years. I am thankful I am still active and able to care for myself. I have been blessed by God.

Age is Relative

Dawn Bechtold

My patient had an unexpected colostomy, secondary to a ruptured diverticulum. The case manager offered the option of home care. My patient's wife was quite surprised that they were offered home care.

She said, "I thought home care was for old people!"

The patient is eighty-two years old.

A True Test of Love

Karen Hopkinson

I fell in love within one week of meeting John at college; we were both twenty years old and attending Marquette University in Milwaukee, Wisconsin. My family lived in Cleveland, Ohio, where I grew up, and after dating for about six months, John wanted to meet my family. My parents and siblings liked John instantly. The day after John arrived, my dad asked me to go for a walk; he wanted to "have a talk."

"Did you tell him about your bag?" he asked me.

"No, I can't; he'll break up with me. He'll be disgusted like everyone else in the world."

When I was ten, I began having frequent episodes of abdominal pain followed by diarrhea. My mother was a nurse and I knew when I told her she would take me to the doctor, so I hid it from her as long as I could. Eventually, she figured out what was going on and took me to the doctor.

I was admitted to the hospital. A week went by and I wasn't getting any better. The doctor told my parents they couldn't handle my case and advised us to go to the Cleveland Clinic where I was diagnosed with ulcerative colitis.

I remember asking my parents who were both crying, "Am I going to stay overnight at this hospital too?" I spent the next six months at the Cleveland Clinic.

I was treated with IV steroids and bowel rest, no food. I was fed with TPN (Total Peripheral Nutrition). A needle was inserted into my neck, near my clavicle. This went on for five months. At that time, I was still having thirty to forty bowel movements a day with blood and mucus. They tried to feed me intermittently, but it was a disaster.

The questions continued, "Mom's going to stay with me, right?"

I got to see her thirty minutes a day. Visiting hours were strict and she was not allowed to stay overnight. Finally I responded to steroids, going into remission for six months when the disease came back with a vengeance. I was re-admitted to the Cleveland Clinic. This time I met with a surgeon, Dr. Fazio.

He said, "The only way I can fix this is to remove the diseased intestines and rectum."

"Please take it out; I can't live like this. How soon can you do this?" I asked.

Then he explained about having an ileostomy and wearing a bag. When he first told me about it, he said that it would be a possibility only and that they would try everything to avoid it.

After the surgeon left, I asked my parents, "Am I going to have a bag hanging off my stomach?"

Dad quickly said no. My mom said there was a real possibility that I would end up with one. My dad couldn't bear to tell me this bad news, but I knew this was exactly what was going to happen. My mom was always the voice of reason.

The surgeon was leaving for vacation and warned that when he got back we might have to do surgery. That night I passed out; my bowel ruptured. The doctor found out when he landed at his destination, got on the next plane, and returned to do the surgery, and I ended up with the bag.

After the surgery, the nurses tried to sit me up in the intensive care unit. They had just put their arms behind my neck and back to prop me up. They wanted me to look at the bag. As I tried to sit up, I looked down at my abdomen and saw my incision open up like a zipper and my bowel came spilling out. My instinct was to grab it to stuff it back in. The nurses screamed at me and told me not to touch the intestine and then placed wet gauze to cover the bowel and held it there. My dad was very scared and started saying a final good-bye as they whisked me back into surgery. He wondered how they could stuff my swollen intestines back into my tiny body.

I came out of surgery with a huge open wound. There were five bumper sutures strapped across the incision with a mesh covering over the fascia with two inches worth of packing, keeping it moist to heal. The nurses taught me how to change the dressing and pack the wound as well as how to change the ostomy bag. The nurses, especially the ostomy nurses were so patient with me and my family. Their compassion and dedication was what inspired me to become a nurse.

That was in 1976, and every year for the next five years, I would get adhesions, which would require surgery to remove the adhesions and ileostomy. I don't tell my patients about that because that is not typical. I don't think it was known at the time, but I played a lot of sports and this may have contributed to the problem along with the fact that my body was still growing.

My dad pressed me further, "You absolutely need to tell John about your ileostomy and tell him tonight."

"He's going to break up with me," I said as I began to cry.

"Maybe he will but he's in love with you at this point, and you can't move forward and not tell him about this. If he can't handle it, he's not the right guy."

"Dad, he is the right guy. I want him to be the right guy."

"Tell him tonight and wake me up when you get home and tell me how it went."

I didn't tell him that night or any night. Six months passed, Thanksgiving passed, and Christmas was around the corner.

I called my parents. "John is coming home with me for Christmas."

My father adamantly said, "No, he's not, unless you tell him about your bag."

John wanted to give me my Christmas gift early, it was a ring, not an engagement one, but it was very pretty. I was shocked.

"This isn't an engagement ring, but I do want to marry you. We both have another year of school and I think we should wait until after that."

I became hysterical. He couldn't understand my reaction. I told him, "I can't marry you, I can't marry anybody."

He asked, "Why? Why?"

"There's a really bad thing about me, really bad, really bad."

"What is it?"

Since I couldn't say anything, he started guessing, "Are you sick?"

"Yeah, really sick, actually no, I was sick…"

He was getting more frustrated, confused, and sad, "Are you married?"

"No, I'm not married."

"Are you gay?"

"No, of course not."

"Are you dying?"

"No, it's way worse than that."

"What could possibly be worse than that?"

"I have this thing, it's the most horrible disgusting thing, you can't even imagine this thing, and it's so bad. It's never going away and it's always going to be a part of me."

He was completely confused, "I don't understand."

"I have this disfiguring thing with my body; it's disgusting, really gross!"

"Can I see it?"

I explained to him, "It's an ileostomy; I have to poop into a bag the rest of my life. Just prepare yourself; this is the absolute worst thing in the world you'll ever see."

"Okay, I'm ready."

Then I showed it to him, "See?"

"That's it? That's the thing?"

"Yeah, isn't it the worst thing in the world you could ever imagine?"

"No, that's not the worst thing. The worst thing in the world would have been if you were born flat-chested. That would have been a problem, the bag… I can deal with."

Then I proposed to him.

Questions
Jocelyn Anderson

My husband and I traveled to the state horseshoe tournament along with our fifteen-year-old grandson who would be pitching horseshoes and staying in our room. I thought, *Even though he knows I have a urostomy(alternate surgical construction needed to eliminate urine), he might get more of an education on this trip.* Since my urostomy night-drainage system can't be hidden, the questions came, "Grandma, do you do that every night?"

"Yes."

"For how long do you have to do it?"

"As long as I live."

I explained everything about my urostomy to him. When I finished, I said, "Maybe you would like to be a nurse, like your uncle."

"No, Grandma, I think I would rather be a plumber."

Same difference, I thought.

O is for Ostomy
Jude Ebbinghaus

My young daughter Alycia seemed unusually sad the day before Easter. We were decorating eggs when she told me that she didn't want me to go into the hospital after the Easter Bunny came. I looked at the fearful expression on her sweet little face and tried to explain to her that I was not going back into the hospital because Dr. Toledo had made me all better. She wasn't buying it, so I decided it was time to give my three-year-old a course in "Ostomy 101."

I took her to the bathroom and propped her up on the counter. I laid out my supplies and explained to her that they were Feldspar's clothes. She asked who Feldspar was, and I told her that Feldspar was my ileostomy. She asked, "What's that?" I said, "Mommy's new poop chute." I then proceeded to show her my belly. I showed her my lifeline and told her that my tummy had been very sick and that Dr. Toledo saved my life by taking the sick part out and sewing up my tummy. I explained that Feldspar had to change clothes just like she did, so I removed my pouch and showed her my stoma. She watched with amazement and broke into giggles when Feldspar started pooping. I quickly cleaned up, put on my new pouching system, and slipped on a Mickey Mouse pouch cover, which she loved and wanted one for herself. I laughed and lifted her down to the floor and asked her what she thought about my ileostomy.

She put her hands on her small little hips, tilted her head, and said, "I think Feldspar has the cutest little poops that I've ever seen!" Then she turned and ran out the door into the playroom.

I stood there amazed at her reaction and thought, *Wow. If only adults could look at their new ostomy through the eyes of a three-year-old, they'd be in such a better place.*

A year later Alycia was in preschool and learning about letters and their sounds. Every night she came home with a homework bag with a letter on it and she was to find things that began with that letter. It was "O" night and she seemed to be stumped. She tried to put her octopus in the bag but it wouldn't fit. She tried other items that began with the letter O, but they just didn't work. She came to me for help, and we read the "Little Miss O" book and then we talked. Suddenly a light went off in her head. You could see the excitement in her eyes as she jumped off my lap and ran.

The next morning as Charlie was packing her lunch, he asked about her homework and she proudly replied that it was done. He asked to see what she had in her "O" bag so she carefully unrolled the flap and pulled out Mommy's "O"stomy pouch. Charlie choked on his coffee, and Alycia asked what was wrong. Trying not to laugh, Charlie tried to explain why she could not take Mommy's ostomy pouch to school. She insisted that ostomy was the perfect "O" to show and tell!

After much discussion, we convinced Alycia to take a jar of olives to show, tell, and share for a snack!

Out of the Mouths of Babes
Joanne Heitzman

A few months after surgery, I got the courage to venture out into the real world again. I have both a colostomy and urostomy, which I must catherize every four hours. I am so grateful just to be alive that I don't worry too much about all the little details and have learned to just go about my own business.

We had lunch out and I had to use the restroom. There, I need to stand facing the bowl to catherize.

A mom came into the stall next to me with her young child.

She said to her little one, "Just stay in here with the door closed." I was hoping the child would not appear underneath the petition.

I broke out laughing when I heard the child ask her Mom, "Why does the lady next door have her shoes on backwards?"

My shoes were facing the toilet rather than away—out of the mouths of babes. Who would ever have thought about it? If I could have, I might have wet my own pants laughing. I learned that you just have to laugh about most things.

An Amazing Lease on Life
K. Ann Hambridge

I looked across the hospital bed at my husband and thought, *here we go again*. His late wife had died after battling cervical cancer for ten years. *Was it my turn now?*

The life changing words came from my colorectal surgeon in 1991, "There's no evidence that you've ever had hemorrhoids, but I want you in here tomorrow for cancer surgery!"

Colon cancer. I'd already had three benign lumpectomies and a hysterectomy due to endometriosis. Could it really be cancer this time? Was this the end of my life? How would I cope? How would he cope?

A necessary colostomy changed my lifestyle, my diet, and my attitude toward life. Each day became a blessing. I visited an elderly friend in the hospital who blurted out, "Ann, I've got a bag!"

Much to her surprise I replied, "Rita, so have I."

From that moment she decided life might be worth living, and if I could survive, so could she, and fifteen years later, she is still enjoying life, grateful for her colostomy.

Sixteen months after my surgery, my husband died. I carried on our franchise coffee business single handedly until it became profitable. Eighteen months after becoming a widow, I got a phone call from a dear, trusted friend of thirty years from across the Atlantic.

"Ann, Nora's died, what do I do now?"

The answer to that was I, this middle-aged grandmother, ran away from home. Romance is remarkably therapeutic. At the age of fifty-three, complete with colostomy, I remarried, left Scotland, and immigrated to Canada to begin a completely new and exciting life in Calgary.

Two months later I knew there was something wrong. I couldn't sit comfortably because of pain in my tailbone, and I felt as if I had hemorrhoids. It took eight months for my medical records to appear from Scotland so the Tom Baker Cancer Centre in Calgary could accept me as a patient. After many tests, a colonoscopy revealed another suspected tumor.

I looked across the hospital bed at my husband of eleven months and thought, *here we go again. His late wife died after battling breast cancer for fourteen years, now it was my turn, again. Colon cancer, again. How would he cope? How would I cope? Had I sold everything, left home, family, and country and come to Canada just to die? No way!*

With excellent surgery, my colostomy was sent into retirement and an ileostomy took its place and brought physical changes. Fiber was difficult to absorb and diarrhea frequent and this forced me to consider how I could help others to accept changed body function and, in some cases, find the will to live.

With my faith background, I was already a qualified pastoral care hospital visitor, so it was a small step to take Calgary Ostomy Society Volunteer Visitor training. As a registered visitor, I have met many people anxious to learn how to cope emotionally as well as with the practicalities of a colostomy or ileostomy.

After visiting with one lady for five minutes she said, "It's okay; I don't need you now! You look normal."

Her fear of looking deformed, tummy bulging, unable to wear normal clothes was allayed by seeing me healthy and smartly dressed with no visible bulges. All sorts of questions have been asked of me. *How do you fart with a pouch? What about intimate relationships? Can we still…?* My answers usually raised a smile.

Despite the surgery, I still couldn't sit comfortably. Sitting in a car, kayak, or on a dining chair all caused me great discomfort. Many tests and six years later, the culprit was identified, a metastatic cancerous colon tumor in my sacrum! Pioneer surgery was performed that involved plastic and urology surgeons. My ileostomy was moved from right front abdomen to left front abdomen. A three-inch wide, eight-inch long band of skin and muscle was loosened and turned inside out to form a new lining for my vagina. After several blockages, I had further surgery in which my bladder was disconnected and I received a urostomy. Now my belly button is three inches left of center and I have freedom from pain. In one twelve-month period, I spent a total of six months in the hospital. Weight loss came with these surgeries, and I discovered that uncushioned seats are extremely hard. As an added bonus, I am qualified to visit urostomy patients in the three Calgary hospitals.

Even though I cannot digest many of the recommended healthy foods, I enjoy many luxuries like chocolate and include an occasional glass of wine. Because of the risk of dehydration through my central line, I infuse two liters of saline solution overnight, every night. Accidents? Of course, and sometimes amusing. One day I didn't leave enough time after lunch for "processing." I was driving on a busy road when my pouch inflated so much that the flange seal came undone. Phew. What a place to have to change a pouch. The policewoman was remarkably understanding even if I was causing an unusual type of blockage. Thanks to my short gut and lack of storage, I have extremely high and frequent output, so often wear a large night ileostomy pouch during the day. One nurse likened it to an elephant's trunk, but it allows me to attend meetings or travel without urgent washroom stops. No one would guess what is hiding under my long flowing skirt.

Surviving three bouts of colon cancer means I enjoy an amazing new lease on life, free of pain. My husband and I have traveled within Canada from Calgary to Victoria in the west and Newfoundland in the east, and to New York, Arizona, Britain, Portugal, Spain, Finland, and Australia. That is a lot of flying. When we travel, most of my baggage is taken up with hydration and ostomy equipment, and clothes are low priority. To facilitate one seven-time-zone journey, my clinic manager suggested I hook up drainage for my urostomy before leaving home, to infuse continuously until arriving in London. That caused an interesting episode when airport security wanted to put the pump through the X-ray machine until I pointed out that it was attached to me so I needed to be put in too.

My surgeon describes me to his students as a miracle. As he operates only on cancer patients no other surgeon will touch, many of his patients don't survive two years. Against all predictions I'm increasingly healthier seven years later and he's discharged me. Previously I was the first patient to graduate from palliative care. While I give him full credit (he keeps his patients morale high by wearing funny hats), he says it's my positive attitude and determination that make the difference.

One of many lessons I have learned is that what may at first appear to be a disaster can be turned into a blessing. Every day I thank God for the wonderful surgical, medical, oncology, and nursing care available. I also am thankful for my supportive husband, loving friends, and for the opportunities I've been given to walk with others. It is a joy to me to share the good news that there is indeed quality life possible after colon cancer. Thanks to the re-plumbing and redesigning my own body has undergone, I no longer have cancer. Love, fun, and laughter make every day worth living.

No Guts
Jill Olson

At twenty years old, after suffering from ulcerative colitis for two years, it became evident that I needed surgery to have my colon removed, which would give me a temporary ileostomy.

The first time I visited my surgeon, he told me a joke and informed me that I needed to tell him a joke sometime. Time went on, I had surgery, and my doctor told me jokes almost every time I saw him, even at 6:00 in the morning in my hospital room.

When I was recuperating, I went to his office for a checkup and finally had a joke for him, a joke that my then three-year-old nephew loved to tell: *Why didn't the skeleton cross the road? Because he had no guts!* Since my doctor is a GI surgeon, it was very fitting. He laughed, praised me for finally telling him a good joke, and it allowed me to see that I could have a sense of humor about the situation.

Also, a short time before I was to have surgery, my mother was discussing it with one of her friends. She told her friend that I was going to have my whole colon removed and her friend said, "Well, she has more guts than I do!"

Mom responded with, "Not for long!"

So it is a big joke in our family that I don't have any guts, but I am proud of it because I feel great. This surgery allowed me to live a normal life and be me again.

Adventures of a Bag Lady
Jocelyn Anderson

I was in one of four buses filled with senior citizens that stopped at a nice restaurant for dinner prior to attending a musical production. After dinner, before leaving for the theater, approximately one hundred people, mostly women, headed for the restrooms. This created a long waiting line at the women's restroom. Noticing there was no line at the men's restroom, I and several other women moved over to that restroom line.

Soon it was my turn to enter. I stepped in and beheld the one and only enclosed stall and three ladies waiting to use it. I observed four urinals so I stepped up to a urinal, took out my urostomy pouch spigot, emptied the pouch, and tucked everything back into my elastic-waist pants. I washed my hands, and told the puzzled waiting ladies, who were strangers to me, "Have a nice day!" and left the restroom.

Running Motivation
Regis DiGiacomo

I have a rare condition called "Fox Den's" disease. It required the removal of part of my colon and my rectum. I now have a colostomy, and I wear a plastic pouch on the right side of my abdomen. The pouch has a drainage opening at the bottom that is secured with a plastic clip. I have had this about ten years.

Mishaps can happen, but they are rare. It doesn't stop me from exercising regularly and strenuously—bicycling and running mainly. Running tends to make the bowels work well, causing my pouch to fill nearly full. While running one morning on my treadmill, the tail closure clip somehow managed to get caught in my running shorts and it was triggered open. Do you know what happens when s--t hits a treadmill belt at six mph? Needless to say, I had quite a cleanup chore.

Another time I was running outside early one morning and had a similar problem when the clip holding the bottom of the pouch closed came loose. I quickly took off my t-shirt to clean my leg. Fortunately it was very early, I don't think I ever ran that fast since and luckily for my neighbors it rained later that morning.

The Foreign News
Lisa Davis

"You will need a permanent ostomy bag." The words hit me like a sledgehammer. There I was in a doctor's office on London's exclusive Harley Street, receiving words I never expected to hear. Only two days before, I received information I never expected to get after a routine colonoscopy. The doctor looked at me with tears in his eyes and said, "We've found cancer."

I thought I had heard him wrong! *I don't have time for cancer!*

I was working at the American embassy in Moscow, Russia, working lots of overtime hours while substituting for the ambassador's secretary, when I realized it was time for my annual physical. As part of the exam, I was given a blood test that showed I was a bit anemic. More blood tests followed and soon it was recommended for me to see a specialist in London.

Whew-hoo! London. A week of living large and going to plays along with just one silly little doctor's appointment squeezed into my social schedule. It was a small price to pay for a free trip for a week. My husband would join me for the weekend, and we had thoughts of a long romantic get away to enjoy ourselves.

It all came to a screeching halt when I got the news from the doctor in London that I had rectal cancer. I was lying on the hospital gurney in London trying to reach my husband at the American embassy in Moscow. At last the Marines were finally able to reach him; God bless those Marines.

Two days later, after wrapping up loose ends, he was on a plane headed to London. After he arrived, we went to the American embassy in London where we were told I would be going to the states for cancer surgery and would not be allowed to return to Moscow. Two hours later, I received the news that I would be getting an ostomy bag. It was such a scary prospect, I had a vague notion of what being an ostomate was all about, but I didn't have any idea exactly how or where the bag would be attached.

It helped me immensely to visit the place in London where ostomy bags were manufactured. I was able to touch and talk about pouches with a wonderful technician. Many of my fears were laid to rest as I realized that ostomy bags were small and lightweight, not big or bulky, as I was afraid they would be.

The rest of the weekend was spent doing tourist stuff, The Eye on London, a kind of gigantic ferris wheel, tea at Harrods, Spamalot—the musical, and lots of sightseeing.

In addition, there were calls back to the states to my poor mother-in-law, who had two days to find a colorectal surgeon. *Where to start?* Fortunately, she contacted a doctor who attended her church, and she was able to get the name of a wonderful surgeon in northwest Arkansas.

Two days later, we left for the states. Shortly after my arrival, pain began along with severe fatigue. I had to travel in the car lying down, because it hurt too badly to sit. The surgeon was able to confirm what the British doctor had found—I indeed had colorectal cancer. Ten days later, I was on an operating table, and nine days following, I left the hospital to recover at home.

Before surgery, I was put in contact with a Wound Ostomy Continent nurse. I didn't even know such heavenly creatures existed. She had me sit, lie down, and twist before she marked the spot where my ostomy would be, and then she attached a bag for practice so I could see what it would be like. My first appointment with her lasted three hours. Thanks to her careful planning, the ostomy was put in a good location, and I have had little trouble with it. But it has been a road to recovery that I am still climbing. There are no local support groups. Through the Internet, I have picked up tips and some things I figured out on my own. My first few bag changes, with my husband's help, took forty-five minutes. Now I do it on my own in less than ten minutes.

I've also picked up tidbits from my nurse such as traveling with a small bottle of water for those occasions when no water may be available. My mom has made me beautiful pouch covers that are pretty enough to wear outside my clothes. What I thought was originally a death sentence. has ended up being an interesting detour on the road to life. I've picked up a new vocabulary and some new perspectives on life. If I, being a self-confirmed klutz, can manage this, I think anyone can!

Pregnant Pause
Jay Pacitti

In March of 2000, my gastroenterologist recommended surgery. Diagnosed with Crohn's disease three months earlier, this was my best chance to find remission and deal with the disease on a level playing field. I would need several inches of my small intestine and colon removed. While getting rid of the diseased bowel was necessary, it was still a nerve-wracking proposition. In the three days before my surgery, I had a colonoscopy, multiple blood tests, and at least one pregnancy test. This made sense to me. I was all for having the surgery team know what to expect when they cut me open.

On the surgery day, I arrived to the hospital in time for my 1:00 p.m. surgery and for the hospital paperwork and prep that would be involved. My supportive partner accompanied me to the hospital, as she had to the surgery consultation. This was a trying time in my life and in our young relationship. Until that time, I had been completely healthy. The Crohn's diagnosis came just a bit over a year into our relationship.

That day, in the hospital, she was understandably nervous—far more than I was. Because I was taking the steps that would lead to my best chance for remission, I didn't feel anxious. What I did feel was hungry.

Colon surgery requires a prep that includes a bowel cleansing routine. I had not eaten or had anything to drink that day and nothing but clear liquids for the prior twenty-four hours. Because I needed a colonoscopy earlier in the week, this meant I did the clear liquid routine twice in five days, which is why I was so hungry.

My surgery time was delayed a couple of times. I sat in an uncomfortable chair in a small room, wearing a hospital gown and watching bad daytime television that featured numerous food commercials. I was tired, hungry, and starting to get pretty punchy.

My partner got more and more nervous with each passing hour. We both knew I was going in for a pretty substantial operation. While I was waiting, they ran a few more tests, including a second pregnancy test of the week—just to make sure.

Finally, around 4:30 p.m., headed in the direction of the operating room, while wearing my flattering hospital gown and paper slippers, we walked down the chilly halls. My partner accompanied me and we were told to wait in an area with a couple of chairs and people in scrubs walking about purposefully. I sat down in a plastic chair in what seemed like the middle of the room and my partner stood right behind me, too nervous to sit. We realized that this was not just a pre-op area; it seemed to have some post-op patients as well. We were surprised that she had been allowed to accompany me into this part of the hospital.

My surgeon came by, apologized for the delay, and promised we'd be going in really soon. A few minutes later, a woman in scrubs wearing a paper surgical cap over her hair and toting a clipboard came to talk to me. I sniffed the air as she neared . . .What was that scent? *Doritos.* My hunger flared as she introduced herself as the anesthesiologist, while she brushed the Dorito crumbs from the corner of her mouth. She apologized for having a snack a minute ago. I told her, "I don't care, I just want some. Now!"

She ignored my attempt at lightening the mood and got down to business. My partner remained standing behind me, distracted and worried as she waited for the surgery to finally commence. The questions began, "Name? Age? Weight? Are you pregnant?"

I laughed. As the anesthesiologist bent over her clipboard, I said, "No, I'm not pregnant. I am 100 percent certain that I am not pregnant. I took a pregnancy test earlier this week. And not only that, they gave me another one this afternoon. So, no, I am not pregnant. And besides, we keep trying, but it just *doesn't seem to work*."

The doctor, intently scribbling down all of my answers to her questions replied. "Well don't give up. You should keep trying. They're getting very good at that stuff now, and you should . . . *glancing up*. . . you should . . . *realization dawning*. . . Oh. You mean you two. That's very funny. I'm going to talk about you while you're asleep!"

Baby Banter

Brenda Elsagher

My sister Chris was in labor and over a lunchtime phone call to her husband, Joe; they agreed he would meet her in two hours to take her to the hospital. She wasn't worried; the hospital shared the same parking lot with the county courthouse where she was employed.

Joe was a teacher at the time and a conscientious one at that. He is a mellow guy, not known for moving too fast, slow and steady most of the time. Joe gave the students his undivided attention and instead of leaving school at the agreed upon hour, he prepared lesson plans for the substitute teacher and assisted some students with homework.

Chris is not known to panic. However, after waiting an hour after the school day was over, she called the school to see what was delaying him; he assured her he would be there momentarily. The school was less than a mile away. He showed up ten minutes later to pick Chris up to head over to the hospital.

As she was about to go down the stairs with Joe at her side, her water broke. It quickly became evident that the hospital may not be an option. Luckily, the sheriff's office was located at the bottom of the open stairway and a lieutenant was in the hall. He assisted Joe and Chris and summoned help from the sheriff's office. The deputies quickly assessed the situation and promptly guarded the doors and entrances in the area. Two public health nurses were alerted and came to assist. Gossip soon spread around the building that a cop had a lady pinned to the floor outside the sheriff's office.

One "ouch," two pushes, and eight minutes since her water broke, the ambulance arrived after driving the entire half block to deliver my beautiful niece Claire. The gathering group sang "Happy Birthday" to Claire while Chris was reminding her fellow employees to change her timecard as she ended up laboring an extra hour!

Courthouse staff suggested the baby be named Courtney, but Joe and Chris opted for Claire, after a beloved great-grandmother. An employee called a local news tip line to report the event. Since it was a slow news day, Claire's birth even made the ten o'clock news. The not-so-funny anchorman commented after the news broadcast that Claire should have been called "Ida Claire" since she was born in a courthouse.

Babies come into our world and we are never the same. Many of the following stories attest to that truth.

Baby, Oh Baby
Laverne Bardy

My girlfriend Carol was looking through the hospital's nursery window. Her daughter, Kathy, had just given birth to a baby girl. It was Carol's first grandchild and she was beside herself with joy.

Standing with Carol was the infant's father, Kenny.

"The baby is absolutely beautiful," Carol said. "She has Kathy's eyes, and Kathy's nose. She even has the same mouth as Kathy."

Kenny stared pensively at his infant daughter. After a long pause he asked, "Doesn't she look anything like me?"

Without missing a beat Carol answered, "Your mother is coming tomorrow; then she'll look like you."

My Magic Shoulder
Judy Epstein

I have a magic shoulder. At least, my toddler thinks so. Any time he falls and hurts himself, or feels tired, or just unhappy, he calls for it.

"Mommy's shoulder!" he sobs, the tears streaming down his face. And when I pick him up and he nestles there, he seems consoled. So I guess it works.

But one of these days, I am sure he'll see right through me. He'll ask for my shoulder, and I'll pick him up and he won't feel any better. What will I do then?

I think I know how it got started. It was the night he got the croup. That horrible night, when I catapulted awake, knowing only that something was wrong. The bed next to me was empty because my husband was already in the baby's room, holding our son while he struggled to breathe. Too panicked to look anything up in the baby books, I rushed them both into the bathroom; turning on both the sink and the shower taps full force and cursing the hot water when the supply ran out. As the steam billowed around us with no discernible effect, Jeff went to get the pediatrician on the phone.

I could hardly even hear my husband shouting at me through the door. "The doctor asked, 'Is he breathing any better?'"

"No!"

"Then we have to go to the emergency room!"

"How? I can't even leave the bathroom to get dressed!"

So my husband brought in some clothes. And through it all, my clinging baby wouldn't go to Daddy long enough for me to fasten my bra, crying pitifully for "Mommy's shoulder." A horrible feeling, my child crying for me, thinking I could make it better. Even more horrible, knowing I couldn't.

As we raced through the night to the hospital, car windows down because the doctor said the cold night air would help (I never thought I'd be happy to see fog!), I kept wondering, *How many minutes do we have? If he stops breathing right now, how long before brain damage begins?* I was so scared, I almost stopped breathing myself.

When we got to the hospital, they brought us right in. The baby refused to sit on the bed and breathe from the tube they handed him—it was hissing something fierce; I think it frightened him—so I stood with it facing him over my shoulder.

After half an hour, we all started breathing a little easier, and my eyes wandered around the room. I looked over at the curtains pulled around the bed. They look familiar. Of course. We've been here before. The same curtains. The same bed. The same shoulder, even.

This same baby was only sixteen days old (and home from the hospital only seven of those days) when he began to run a fever. After a day full of uncharacteristic fussing, his temperature went up to 100.5° F. That was when the pediatrician said we had to bring him in to the emergency room, where, ultimately, they did a spinal tap and then admitted him, for a few days of intravenous antibiotics to make sure he didn't have meningitis.

My mother was still staying with us at that point, so she went with us on that trip to the emergency room. And I was glad she was there—especially when the nurse started barking questions at us. "What is the baby's name? His age? His most recent temperature?" My husband, my mother, and I all spoke at once, "100 point 5." Clearly impatient with the confusion, the nurse barked again. "MOM, what was the baby's last temperature?"

There was a silence. I looked up at my mom, waiting for her to speak. But then I realized that everyone else was looking at me. Oh. I was "Mom." They meant *me*!

I hardly had time for the revelation to sink in before the nurse started barking again. Only the baby's parents could stay with him, she said; my mother would have to go out to the waiting room.

My mother must have caught the panic in my voice as I asked, "Do you have to go?" She gave me a little hug, and said, "It'll be all right." And I didn't think, *How does she know that?* I just felt better.

Remembering that, I relaxed. "Mommy's shoulder" would work this time. It would always work. How do I know? Easy—it's magic.

He Must Be Adopted

Joan Clayton

Our son had an unusual birth. The minute his little head was born, I heard a soft peaceful cry, yet I felt his body still within me. Such an awesome feeling made me think no one in the whole world had ever done that before. Eight pounds and twenty-two inches in length, I predicted in my heart that he would be tall, dark, and handsome, just like his daddy.

Of course, every mother thinks her baby is the prettiest, and I was no exception. People stopped me to marvel at my baby. At six months, Lance cooed and laughed at everyone. Even the pediatrician said, "Yes, he's a fine baby and handsome too!"

At eight months old, Lance had a strep throat and had to be hospitalized. I was up all night rocking, walking, and soothing as best I could. The nurse's shift at seven o'clock the next morning brought a newly employed nurse. I'm sure I looked bedraggled with no hairdo, no make-up, and no sleep.

She walked in with her chart and looked at Lance and then me. She instantly gasped while saying, "What a beautiful baby. He must be adopted!"

The Baby and the Blue Suede Shoes
Linda O'Connell

Elvis Presley swiveled his hips and wailed about his blue suede shoes.

I know exactly how he felt. I loved my blue suede slip-on shoes with rounded toes and low heels. They had a tiny little floral die-cut design across the top, the only pair of flats that actually fit my swollen feet comfortably when I was pregnant with my son. I swore I would never throw them away; I planned to have them resoled if my toes poked through the leather soles, but I drastically changed my mind about that when I went into labor.

I was completely in control of my breathing. I harnessed the contractions as fast as they came and rode them like a wild stallion. It was my mother and mother-in-law riding in the back seat on the way to the hospital who made me want to scream. They hissed at my former husband to hurry, insisting he blow through red lights, swore they'd pay the speeding ticket or talk the police officer out of issuing one if we got pulled over. Where is a cop when you need one? If only he could lock these grandmas up or paddy wagon them back to their own homes.

What were we thinking making this a family affair? I wondered.

When we arrived at the hospital, the orderly with his prize fighter muscles and more gold in his grin than I had on my left hand, placed me in a wheelchair and told the nurse to call housekeeping.

"Got to get that stream cleaned up." That trickle trailed us all the way off the elevator.

"This mamma's got a big bag of waters," he said in his baritone voice. "A'fore long, fish'll be swimming in the puddle."

If he'd been standing in front of me I'd have tripped him with my blue suede beauties. *Maybe he'll slip in midstream!*

A lanky, veteran nurse walked in my room with untamed, wiry, gray hair and milk-pale skin. She quashed my malevolent thoughts with her no-nonsense attitude. "Stand up now, little mother, we have to get you into a gown."

She stuck her thumbs in her waist band, hiked her pants, sniffed, and helped me up. Another trickle, then a gush of amniotic fluid sloshed down my legs and filled my lovely shoes.

"My shoes are ruined," I cried.

"Don't worry about your shoes, sit on the bed. I'll help you take them off."

She pulled on a pair of latex gloves. Her right hand was missing two digits, the middle and ring finger. She looked like she was signing I love you in American Sign Language.

"You having back labor? I can give you a back rub," she said as she lifted my leg and tugged at my shoe.

Ain't no way, sister! I thought.

She tugged harder, "What did you do, buy these before you were pregnant?"

I wanted to kick her, but she had an eight-finger grip on my leg that could have snapped it in two. On the third tug, she finally pried the shrunken wet shoes off my feet.

Her startled, wide-eyed expression frightened me more than her gasp.

"Oh my, oh dear—you having a hard time breathing, sweetie?"

Was she kidding me? I'd had difficulty breathing ever since this tub of lard kid shoved my diaphragm into my throat.

She blinded me with her pen light. "Dilating," she said.

My eyes or my cervix?

With concern she said to an aide, "We need an oxygen reading on her—look!" She pointed at my feet. *Is the baby lying in my shoe? Fish floating? Ankles ballooned and ready to burst?*

"What's wrong?" I asked.

"Don't worry. You just slide on back in that bed until we can hook you up to the monitors and get your doctor in here to see this."

My obstetrician bustled into the room.

"Looks like we're going to have a baby. Scoot down so I can examine you."

"No—uh-uh." I snapped my head left and right and held tight as he tried to lift the sheet.

"What do you mean? There's no turning back now. Let me take a look."

"No, I can't."

He untucked the sheets, pruned up his face, and mumbled, "Oh my—my goodness."

I transferred from the gurney to the delivery table. The labor pains were nothing compared to the agony I felt when I saw what had made the doctor and attendants gasp. One moment my pink, plump, piggies were in my beloved blue suede shoes and the next moment my raisin-wrinkled, blue-stained feet were in the stirrups.

Next the doctor said, "Okay, push! Here comes your baby!"

Most expectant mothers strive to get a glimpse of their newborn entering the world. I was too distracted by my own feet!

An Alien Inside Me

Ginger Truitt

It's been fourteen years since my last pregnancy and, being fairly naïve, I still learned new things about my body each day. After my last OB/GYN appointment, I wondered how the doctor measuring my belly could tell exactly how pregnant I was. Two days later, lying on my bed, I began to sit up and noticed a giant thing bulging out of my abdomen. I nudged my husband, pointed, and said, "Either I have an alien growing inside me or I just found my uterus."

He gave my belly a glance and groggily replied, "Well, it's something."

I repeatedly lifted myself to a partially reclining position, watching the bulge go in and out, "That's amazing, there's a baby in there!"

"Uh-huh," my sleepy husband replied, hoping for five more minutes of sleep before the alarm clock jangled.

Over the next several days I was fascinated by the bulge, lying on the floor as I watched it pop out. I'd talk to it, push it around and try to make the baby kick. I wondered why I had a bulge with this pregnancy, why was this different? Gifted with an active imagination, I realized that the bulge wasn't my uterus, but I decided it was a cancerous tumor. I found myself praying through my tears to deliver a healthy baby.

The next day I sought the doctor and found out I had rectus diaphysis, a hernia five inches long and three inches wide. During my visit, word reached the hallway that this pregnant woman had a little something extra growing out of her belly. Soon, another nurse, the nurse practitioner, and the receptionist all came in to peek at my freakish bulge.

At home, I milked it for all it was worth. If I wanted someone to carry a laundry basket for me, I'd pop out my bulge saying, "I wish I could carry this but my rectus diaphysis is killing me."

The kids were fascinated with the hernia, especially when I explained it's actually my intestines popping through an opening in my muscle. Having seen science fiction movies, they think it's cool that Mom can make her abdomen look like an alien is about to pop out of it. Even my husband has some pride in the hernia. One Sunday morning at church he patted my belly and said with pride, "Show 'em your alien, Honey."

"I can't show them my alien unless I lie down and pull up my shirt!" Everywhere else I went, I was a regular sideshow freak. The girls in my husband's office enjoyed it, the folks at our bluegrass jam got a kick out of it and with some minor prompting, I almost felt like hopping on the conveyor belt check out at Wal-Mart. I hope the baby never finds out that people were more excited about my hernia than they were the pregnancy. It might cause him to grow up feeling a little alienated.

Baby's First Ride Through the Car Wash

Carol Gustke

It was February 1, and freezing rain pelted the windows of our warm cozy bungalow. We cuddled in front of the blazing fireplace, drinking hot cocoa. At nine-and-a-half months pregnant, my belly was my tray. Suddenly, an intense cramp wrapped itself around my massive mound of stretched flesh, and s-q-u-e-e-z-e-d. The cup of cocoa tumbled to the floor as I gasped for air.

My husband bolted upright. "What's wrong?"

When I was able to speak, I inched out the word, "Contraction, con-traaaction." It was like saying, "Sick-um to a pitbull."

My husband raced to the closet, grabbed his coat, and slammed the front door behind him. Moments later, he returned.

"Let's go, let's go," he said, and pulled me from the chair.

"Go where?" I asked.

"To the hospital. The car is running."

"I'm not going anywhere," I shot back. "All I had was one contraction."

Just then, another gut-wrenching cramp doubled me over.

"That's two," shouted my husband.

"I can count," I said between clenched teeth.

"Well, I'm not delivering this baby! I'm calling the doctor."

There was no point in arguing with him. I eased myself onto the couch and waited.

"Uh-huh, uh-huh." I heard bits and pieces of the conversation. Moments later, my husband returned.

"Doc says to come in, but there's no hurry since this is our first. Still, I'm concerned about the roads."

I agreed, and minutes later we were on our way. Thankfully, the hospital was only two blocks away. Just before arriving, my husband made an abrupt turn and headed down another street.

"Where you going?" I asked.

He gave a sheepish grin. "To the car wash."

"The car wash! Aren't you the one who was hell-bent on getting to the hospital?"

"I know, I know, but this will only take a minute. I don't want all this ice build-up on the car."

We entered the car wash just as a contraction hit. I couldn't get out and I couldn't stand up.

"Ohhhh," I moaned.

The long arms of rags slapped against the windows as the car rocked back and forth toward the exit. Another contraction hit, then another. I could envision the headlines, "Wife shoots husband in car wash." No two ways about it, I'd be acquitted.

At last, entering the hospital, I collapsed into a wheelchair and was whisked to the labor room. Five hours later, the doctor held up a beautiful, blue-eyed boy and said, "That's the cleanest baby I've ever seen."

Can You Top This? Please Don't!

Judy Epstein

When I came home from the hospital, I was so weak I couldn't lift my own purse, but I had to pick up the phone and call my old roommate from college.

"Hello, Annette. You won't believe where I've been. I've been in the intensive care unit for the past seven days!"

"Whatever happened?"

"Well, after the C-section, I developed a low fever, that turned into a high fever that turned out to be toxic shock syndrome. The baby's fine, but they had me in the emergency room and everything, and then the ICU. It was pretty severe for a while."

I waited for her to exclaim "That's horrible!" or "I don't believe it!" Or, best of all, "Tell me more!" But instead, I heard the following, "Oh, yes, the same thing happened to my sister, only worse. SHE had..."

But I quit listening. I should have known this would happen. After all, I had quit rooming with her in college because no matter what happened to you, she'd had it, too, only more so. If two guys asked you out for the same night, then she'd been asked by the whole fraternity. If you got an A on a paper, then her professor asked permission to publish hers. And when she had her baby, she didn't just have a C-section; she almost died.

Now, here I really had almost died—and with no one to tell!

My husband couldn't bear to listen, he'd been there the first time, and besides, anytime I tried, he corrected me on the details. "Your temperature was never 105 degrees, Judy, it was only 104.6, and you were shivering hard, but you didn't fall out of the bed."

My parents sure didn't want to hear about it—they had already heard it all, and were just glad it was over.

Not even my obstetrician would listen. "Why is it you women always want to tell your horrendous birth stories? I gave a talk on health care last night, but that's all that anyone who came up afterwards wanted to do. I don't get it—if it's such a horrendous experience, why keep bringing it up?"

The thing is, you *need* to talk about these things for a while, before you can get them out of your system.

And it isn't just labor. My father recently went through some hair-raising surgery of his own. He couldn't wait 'til he was well enough to rejoin the monthly poker crew. "All I went in for was a check-up," he told them, "and they wouldn't let me out of the hospital. Wouldn't let another hour go by; just sent me right up for a seven-way bypass!"

"That's nothing, John. Morty here needed eight—didn't you, Mort?"

"Yeah, and they took out a piece of my liver while they were there."

You see. It's hopeless. It's got to be one of the strongest primordial urges, talking about something you've just been through. In fact, there's only one urge stronger—the urge by somebody else to top you.

I decided I'd have to start therapy to find an audience, when the phone rang. It was a neighbor.

"Judy, I heard you almost died having the baby. Are you all right? Tell me all about it!" And you know what? She *listened*.

She called again, a week later. "You'll never believe what happened to me today," she began. "I was in the car, waiting at a light, when all of sudden someone hit me from behind. I looked around and you'll never guess who it was... a police car!"

"That's nothing," I started to say. I know someone who watched at an intersection as two police cars hit each other, each going the wrong way on a one-way street.

But I didn't tell her. "That's terrible!" I said, instead. "What did you do?" Because after all, one good listener deserves another.

Jacob's Birthday
Sari Jo Legge

It was time for my "happy boating accident" to be born. At age thirty-one, I got pregnant through two forms of birth control after years of hoping I could have a child. My Crohn's disease was ruinous to my body through puberty and my twenties. I didn't think I would be gifted with the honor of raising a child. Somehow, I knew this was my only chance to be pregnant.

As my child grew within me, he took the opportunity to use available space on my pelvic floor, previously used by my colon. He had a condo in there and didn't want to leave when the time came. Giving birth to Jacob took away the last vestiges of modesty I was holding onto after years of being the bug on the bed for teaching hospitals to ogle over. As most parents will confirm, labor day is about how many strangers see your entire lady business and how many of those people introduce themselves by rotating their digits in your birth canal. I told them a simple handshake would be more polite, but no one listened.

After a glowing pregnancy with no ileostomy or Crohn's issues, my water broke—all over the bed, floor, and car. We got to the hospital at 10:00 a.m. with our labor coach and friend, Becky, and got settled into our birthing suite at the hospital.

The day started out with a laugh. Becky and I were settling into our room when one of the excellent labor nurses came in to greet us and get some stats. She was carrying my considerable hospital file on a cart. This hospital was the landing zone for most of my Crohn's needs beginning twenty-five years ago. With all these files, you'd have thought she may have read the top couple pages.

In 1987, I had a total proctocolectomy. For all intents and purposes, I have a Barbie butt, just a seam.

The nurse came into our room with a cheery greeting to make us feel confident. The joke was on her. She said to Becky and me, "I see Sari has quite the history of Crohn's disease. I think for the comfort of labor, we'll give you an enema so that you are cleared out. Believe me; it makes things a lot easier!"

Becky and I looked at each other and she winked at me. I nodded. Best friend telepathy. I had been lying on the bed, so I deftly flipped over whilst lifting away the hospital gown to reveal my sewn up ex-dunghole as I said, "If you think you can, give it your best shot, darlin'!"

The nurse went several shades of red as Becky and I were trying to hold our giggles, but the nurse joined in and we all laughed ourselves silly.

The Pitocin drip was started at 1:00 p.m. and from then on all I had was back labor. Only the back of my head and the heels of my feet touched the bed until 6:00 p.m. that night when the epidural was placed.

I have commiserated with other women on how they nearly popped their eyeballs out of the sockets from pushing a child out when your body is numb from the tits down! Your face is the only way to measure the pushing pressure while giving vaginal birth!

Jake took seventeen hours to appear without a cesarean section, but with a one-hundred-suture vaginal section. Becky reported that at no time did I use foul language at anyone; however, I was dropping enough F-bombs to satisfy the biker crowds at Sturgis. At one point, I told the doctor that if he put his hand up me one more time and didn't have Jake with him, he would not get his hand back. I have excellent muscle structure from years of Crohn's clenching to hold back accidents. When my colon was removed, I transferred talent up to the front loader. I am proud to say I am capable of choking a small animal with my Who-Hah, should that ever become necessary. We camp a lot as a family, so I like to be prepared.

Giving birth was scary, wonderful, emotional, and painful; it was miraculous and remains the best thing I ever did. The day remains clear in my mind; I still contend that children should give their mothers gifts for birthday presents instead of the other way around. I knew Jake's day of entry would be like no other day or hospital experience I'd ever had before.

And bless that nurse for staying for the whole seventeen hours, well after she should have clocked out. She was at our side giving us her loving best skill right up until Jake's birth at 12:04 a.m. January 25, 1993. Until Jake and I went home, she came to see to us every day. Laughter really is the best medicine.

Cherry Ames, RN

Carol McAdoo Rehme

"Hold him like a football," the night nurse coached in the dimly lit room. "He's practically as round as one!"

She tucked the whopping ten-pounder under my arm and positioned him to nurse from an engorged breast.

"Latch on there, tanker. Even someone your size needs to eat," she coaxed. With gentle patience, she helped me—helped us.

The mantle of motherhood was crisp and new and perched awkwardly on my shoulders. I looked at her uncertainly. "Like this?"

"Exactly! You're doing great," she praised. Patting my arm, she rose to leave.

"Thank you for your help." I clutched my newborn closer and jiggled his feet to keep him awake as she'd instructed. "What's your name?"

"Call me Cherry," she smiled and headed down the hall to another patient.

Cherry, I grinned down at my son. *I think I've met Cherry Ames, at last!*

Like many adolescent girls in the 1950s and 60s, I devoured books. Especially the fictional series starring a spunky young nurse named Cherry Ames. I admired her unflinching spirit and envied her noble career, her passport to adventure. Cherry was clever, bright, professional.

I loved and knew Cherry Ames. After all, I followed this mystery-solving job-hopper through all twenty-seven books: Student Nurse, Senior Nurse, Chief Nurse. I lived vicariously through her stints as Flight Nurse, Cruise Nurse, and, yes, even Dude Ranch Nurse. Name a place that could possibly use medical care and Cherry was bound to make an appearance—from the mundane rest home, department store, or boarding school, to the exotic jungle, ski lodge, or tropical island.

A couple of my friends, enamored by the romance of Cherry's escapades, set their sights and their hearts on following in her footsteps. They would grow up to be nurses, just like her.

Me? I took one look at my younger sister's compound fracture, flinched, and moved on. To another series: Nancy Drew, spunky young sleuth. But Cherry left her mark on me. I'd know her anywhere.

In fact, I entrusted her once with my croupy toddler in the emergency room. Another time, she dispensed daily allergy treatments at school to my asthmatic daughter. Cherry Ames cried over my teenager in the burn unit each time she debrided him. She appeared—steady, reliable, and speaking Korean—in the trauma unit where my son lay, tethered to life support. And she embraced my heaving shoulders against her warmth until the measured beats of her heart soothed my shock at the sudden death of my dad.

No matter what has happened, Cherry's been there—to dispense vaccinations along with sound advice. To remove casts along with insecurities, to change our dressings, and to change our lives.

Even now, she continues to show up in all sorts of places. Sometimes she's an older, middle-aged, version of herself, sort of like me. Sometimes, she masquerades as a nurturing male. Still, I always recognize her. Just yesterday, I saw her eager reflection in the bright eyes of a newly-minted LPN at the long-term care center where my mother-in-law resides.

Ah, Cherry Ames, RN.

I still love you, Cherry! You've touched my life for decades. And I'm grateful so many young girls grew up to be just like you.

9

Cancer Clarity

Brenda Elsagher

When I was diagnosed with cancer of the rectum at age thirty-nine in 1995, it was a major day wrecker to say the least. I had gone into the clinic that day with my husband, two children—John, age five, and Jehan, age three. My husband, Bahgat (pronounced like a French baguette), had a mole on his forehead that he wanted removed, my son was being tested for strep throat, and my daughter was along for the ride. Most families have fun outings like sliding at the park or McDonald's play land—our outing was a trip to the clinic! I fully expected to walk out that day knowing I would need hemorrhoid surgery, but instead found out I needed surgery to save my life.

Over the next three weeks I had ten different vaginal and rectal exams by ten different doctors, chest X-rays, CAT scans, blood tests, ultra sounds, and more. I didn't have time for cancer, I owned a successful hair salon, was a busy mom, and no one in my family had a history of cancer. I knew people got cancer all the time; I just didn't expect colon cancer, or the other names—colorectal cancer or cancer of the rectum. It was all the same thing, which I didn't know until I educated myself. Up to that point I had totally taken my colon for granted. I never had bowel issues prior, no intestinal diseases except for the occasional bowel changes after traveling in foreign lands.

Now I was forced to learn about the colon and that I would need to have the diseased part of my body, the rectum, that held a golf-ball-sized tumor, removed as soon as possible. I remember asking the doctor after he explained my rectum would have to be removed, "But, don't you need your rectum?" He began to explain I would need a permanent colostomy, vaginal reconstruction, and a hysterectomy and that was the good news! If the cancer had spread, they wouldn't do the operation, but make me as comfortable as they could. All of a sudden, the colostomy looked like a small price to pay for saving my life and to be able to see my children grow up.

That was in 1995, and I wrote about it in detail in my first book, *If the Battle is Over, Why am I Still in Uniform?* I was one of the fortunate ones. The cancer was caught early enough to save my life. I've had some friends since then that were not so lucky. I made a pact with myself from the onset that I would not be embarrassed by what I was dealing with in terms of the physical changes. I knew thousands of people, yet at that time, I didn't know anyone who had colon cancer or even bowel issues. It was such an intensely private subject. With determination, I decided to be vocal about my experience because I found out that colon cancer was the most treatable and preventable form of cancer, with a simple colon cancer screening test called a colonoscopy. Everyone at age fifty and over should have one done and if you have rectal bleeding or bowel changes before that age, see your doctor and schedule a full colonoscopy.

Ironically, having colon cancer spurted me on to doing things I had long put off—learning to be a comic, and attending college. Over the years, I have come to see that cancer wasn't a gift, but finding out that I could deal with a life threatening crisis with a positive outlook, inner strength, honesty, and determination became the gift. We have a choice how we are going to deal with life's challenges. Be proactive, get your colonoscopy today.

Each person dealing with cancer and other life threatening diseases seems to get some introspection to their lives as a gift. We make new choices, appreciate our loved ones more, and laugh more often as you'll find in this next collection of stories.

The Sound of One Kid Laughing
Craig Hergert

Three weeks into my first year of college in the fall of 1974, I was diagnosed with malignant melanoma, an often-fatal form of cancer. Now, I had heard that first quarter could be tough, but I didn't think it would be *you-might-find-out-you-have-cancer* tough. And I knew there'd be tests, but I didn't know they'd include a spinal tap. (Ten years later, when I saw Rob Reiner's film, I knew why he'd given the heavy metal band that name: Their music hurt exactly as much as that test did.)

Once the diagnosis was made, I was sent to a hospital. But not just any hospital: *Children's* Hospital, in Minneapolis. Although I was given excellent care, the whole situation screamed culture shock. A month earlier, I was expecting deep discussions, the possibility of romance, and the certainty of keggers. And just like that, I had a six-year-old roommate. The college brochure had said nothing about this.

I can't remember his name, but I remember he was pretty rowdy that first day. He'd laugh and yell and scream as if he were at a summer camp. And then, the next morning, back from surgery, all he did was yell and scream. I never learned what his problem was exactly, but there had evidently been extensive surgery done on his mouth. As a result, that night was a restless one for both of us.

But what I remember most about my unfortunate roomie was what his dad had done for him. That first day, before his surgery, the nurses had shown him the tape player his dad had provided him, with one children's song after another, sung by none other than my roomie's dad—who, I should point out, was no Frank Sinatra. By that second day, this kid wasn't laughing, but I do remember the nurses getting a kick out of this verse from "Pink Pajamas": "I wear my pink pajamas in the summer when it's hot/And I wear my flannel nightie in the winter when it's not/And sometimes in the springtime and sometimes in the fall/I jump between the sheets with nothing on at all!" So even though this kid wasn't physically able to laugh after his surgery, I think his father's instincts were right. And consider the old vaudeville exchange about offering chicken soup to someone who's dying: "Will that help?" "Couldn't hurt!"

My own rough period at Children's was still to come, and it would bring with it my own experience with what humor can do for a patient. I'd had my first surgery on my second day, which involved removing a cancerous mole from my left ear and a tumor from the base of my neck, and neither of these surgeries had hampered me much. But in the middle of that week, the doctors informed me they'd decided to do a radical neck surgery—a term my Republican dad couldn't have been too happy about—to be sure the cancer hadn't spread into my lymph system. After that surgery, which was performed on Friday, I was nearly as devastated as my young roommate. In a room by myself now, and with sandbags propped on both sides of my head to keep it straight, I watched television mindlessly.

Until Tuesday night. That was the night when something on television would get through to me at Children's. It was 10:30, and I was fully expecting another mindless, restless night. But I happened upon *Candid Camera* on ABC—these were the dark days when there were only four channels to choose from, which that night included a *Candid Camera* classic from the fifties. The segment began with Durwood Kirby sharing a letter from a woman who had noticed that her infant grandson displayed signs of natural rhythm, and she wondered if the *Candid Camera* crew could put that to use. Based on her suggestion, they filmed a number of infants (who appeared to be reaching out toward an off-camera mobile), and set them perfectly to the tune of Beethoven's *Fifth Symphony* so that the babies appeared to be conducting.

Immediately, I did something that I hadn't done for a full week: I laughed out loud. And I mean *LOUD*. It turned out to be so loud that the nurse on duty ran into my room and asked, "What's wrong?" I said, "Nothing, look!" And I pointed toward the screen.

I think that answer is worth a closer look. A nurse asked an eighteen-year-old who had recently been diagnosed with cancer "What's wrong?" and he replied, "Nothing!" And had that question been part of one of my exams at Concordia, I believe it would have been called correct. At that moment, responding fully to the comedy on television, nothing was wrong. I would learn years later, while reading about Norman Cousins' experience in using humor to deal with what had been diagnosed as a terminal illness, that it is impossible to experience laughter and pain simultaneously. Laughter, it turns out, trumps pain. I experienced that for myself that Tuesday night at Children's.

My stay at Children's lasted two weeks, but that lesson lasted much longer. After returning to Minneapolis in 1994, I started doing standup and, within a couple of years, I produced a showcase at Acme Comedy Company. Eager to produce another one, I sought out an organization devoted to helping cancer patients. In the spring of 1997, I found out about The Cancer Kids Fund that meets the non-medical needs of cancer patients at Children's.

Every year since then, I've produced The Cancer Kids Fund Comedy Showcase and Silent Auction in order to help other young patients. Our event has since changed its time of year (it's October now) and its location (the Brave New Workshop), but our purpose remains the same: to make audiences laugh even as we raise money to help young people live to laugh another day.

The best sound in a hospital is the sound of one kid laughing.

Cancer Fighters Laugh
Kay Mickel

People who don't have cancer probably think there's nothing funny about it, but in hospitals and infusion centers around the globe, some people find a way to laugh. The humility of us humans fighting for our lives sometimes propels us to find a giggle hidden within a cloud of gray while we desperately seek to normalize a life that is no longer normal. I have stage 3C ovarian cancer and most days, even I can still find something to laugh about.

We laughed when the breast cancer fighter shared the reason she doesn't wear a breast prosthesis; one time it fell into the oven when she was baking and cookies are more important to her recovery than fake boobs. We laughed with the ovarian cancer fighter with a colostomy who shared about having a blow-out at Wal-Mart; it makes my blow-outs around the house seem tolerable. We women laugh more, maybe because we've always shared a lot.

My husband and I appreciate one another more these days—time is precious. I have formed a committee of my closest friends, male and female, whose job it will be to keep him from getting remarried for at least a year after I'm gone. After that, they should find him what my little niece Sarah calls, a "hottie" who can cook, loves football, and NASCAR.

After a post-op visit at Stanford Cancer Clinic, I was glad to get my Foley catheter removed. It had been my constant companion for over three months and I was sick of it. Because we live over three hours away from Stanford, the doctor wanted us to stay around the clinic, which is connected to the Medical Center, until he knew that I could urinate on my own. Sometimes there is nerve damage, and we needed to know if there was a problem before we left town. Freed from the catheter bag, we strolled across the campus to the cafeteria for lunch, and I drank water—lots of water.

We slowly walked back toward the clinic and sat for a while in the lounge, listening to a volunteer play the grand piano. I felt the urge come to try going without the Foley and I went to the nearby restroom to try it out. It was a state of the art restroom complete with automatic paper towel dispensers and motion sensing toilets that flushed automatically. I was wearing a loose, shift-type dress that day. The deluxe accommodations had seat protective paper that I pulled from the dispenser, tore away the perforations, and placed it on the seat with the flap down in the bowl. Then I turned around, pulled up my shift and, just as I was about to sit, the toilet flushed and the toilet seat paper was whisked away—fast. This happened twice more before I had enough sense to hike my shift up to my armpits and then put the flap of the toilet seat paper outside of the bowl before turning around to sit down.

By this time I really had to go. I made it just in time; my wonderful body remembered how to function on its own. "Hallelujah, thank you, Jesus!" burst forth from me out loud. I half expected there to be another woman in a nearby stall shouting out, "Amen, Sister!" Yes, it's good to laugh.

Hey, Sailor
Mortimer Brown

We were at a meeting of a support group focused on CRF, cancer related fatigue. We were a group of survivors of several forms of cancer. The topic of the discussion was getting more comfortable and beginning to accept our new body as a result of surgery. A woman got up to speak.

"After my mastectomy, I had a very hard time believing my husband could accept me like before. Even though I knew he loved me, I felt sure that my missing breast and missing hair from chemo treatments would turn him off from me when it came to making love. His reassurances to the contrary were taken by me to be just talk. But after hearing some of the stories from y'all here in our meetings, I got to thinking, *maybe it's really me*. So here's what I did. One night he was in the shower while I was taking off my make-up at the bathroom sink. I was feeling a little randy, and decided it was time to take the chance. I called out, 'Hey sailor, how'd you like to make out with a one-titted, bald babe?' At the same time I threw my prosthesis over the top of the shower door."

"Well, in a second, he was out of the shower stall, grabbed me, and together we went back into the shower. That was four nights ago; and we haven't missed a night since."

The applause from our group of twelve could have been mistaken for an ovation from a thousand.

Surrounded by Support

Vince Hopkins

"I'm afraid the biopsy indicates you have non-Hodgkin's lymphoma (NHL)."

And with that short sentence my life was changed forever. The date was October 4, 2005, just twenty days shy of my forty-seventh birthday.

Several months earlier I had noticed a large lump in my neck while shaving. At first I didn't think much of it; it didn't hurt and seemed to have appeared almost overnight. But when it was still there six weeks later, I thought it was time to have the doctor take a look. I went through a series of tests and eventually was referred to an ear, nose, and throat specialist. He took one look at the lump and said it would be best to remove it and do a biopsy. He was pretty sure we were dealing with a swollen lymph node and the obvious concern was it could be lymphoma. The mass was removed on September 28, and seven days later I received the worst possible news.

The doctor immediately assured me that I was not receiving a death sentence, but it was difficult to think of it any other way. Seven years earlier, my wife's brother had been diagnosed with NHL, and after fighting the disease for nearly a year, he passed away as a result of complications due to his treatment. As the news was being delivered, we obviously thought about the worst case scenario. My wife broke down crying while I just sat there, stunned and in disbelief that this was happening to our family again.

The doctor talked with us for a few minutes, but I don't recall much of what he said. He referred us to a couple of oncologists, but due to my involvement with the Leukemia and Lymphoma Society, I told him I would probably ask them to recommend a doctor for me to see. He said we could stay as long as we wanted and once we had composed ourselves, he wished us God's blessings and sent us on our way.

October 4, 2005, was a beautiful day. Birds were singing in the trees and even though it seemed like our world had come to a screeching halt, I realized that life was continuing to go on all around us. I can't explain how angry this made me feel. I thought it was unfair. Out on the street people were driving by without a care in the world, and I had to go home and tell my three children that I had cancer.

There was also another person whom we had to tell—my mother-in-law. She was in poor health herself and had spent the previous weeks in a hospice care facility. She had been diagnosed with lung cancer a couple months earlier, and following surgery to remove a large portion of one of her lungs, had come to the conclusion that she didn't have the strength to fight back. What amazed the family was how at peace she was with her situation. As my wife's sister put it, "She taught us how to live, and she's teaching us how to die."

My wife and I had driven to the doctor's office separately so we gave each other a hug and headed home to talk with our kids. As I was getting into my car, my thoughts drifted to a line from the movie, *The Shawshank Redemption*. Morgan Freeman's character says, "Get busy living or get busy dying."

I realized that I was at a similar point in my life. I could resign myself to the fact that I had cancer, feel sorry for myself, and let this worthless disease beat me, or I could do what was necessary to get better and live my life. It was in God's hands anyway. I had no control over what was going on inside my body, but I could control my attitude. None of us knows how long we'll be here so we might as well live. I didn't want people feeling sorry for me, and I didn't want our house to be like a morgue. I wanted our family life to go on as normal as possible. When we had to do things to deal with the cancer, we'd deal with it and move on.

This doesn't mean there weren't many anxious moments. Telling our kids about my diagnosis was the most painful thing I've ever had to do. It hurt to see them in such pain. Once we got through the initial shock of the situation, they were champs. They helped keep things light around the house, they spent time entertaining me, they helped me continue to live, along with many of our family members and friends. They were all such an inspiration to me and no one was more inspiring than my mother-in-law.

The day after my diagnosis, we went to visit her in hospice. She was bedridden for several weeks and had not been eating, but when we walked into her room, she was sitting up in a chair and eating a sandwich. I looked at her, she looked back at me, and we both grinned. The look on her face told me she had decided to live, and it affirmed my thoughts from the day before about my own situation—I needed to get busy living. She didn't say a word initially, but I knew in her heart she was thinking, *don't worry; we're both going to get through this.* That was almost three years ago and we're both still here today.

What I've shared covers just the beginning of the second part of my life. I had nearly forty-seven years without cancer and just passed the third year anniversary of my diagnosis. I've been cancer free since April 2006, but I realize there is always a chance it could return. That doesn't stop me from living—it makes me want to live more.

I've talked with numerous other cancer survivors and it amazes me how many of them believe their cancer was a blessing. I'll admit I haven't arrived at that point and doubt I ever will. Cancer never has been, and never will be, a blessing to me. But it has made me realize just how blessed I am. I have a wonderful wife, beautiful children, a loving family, and caring friends. I was blessed to receive tremendous care from many outstanding doctors. And I've been blessed to realize what an incredible gift life offers. I guess you really don't know what you have until you're faced with the possibility of losing it all. But I think the biggest blessing through all this has been my mother-in-law, Vivian Riestenberg. Here was a woman who was at peace and prepared to die, but instead she showed me how to fight back. She inspired me like no one else.

Many of our family members have said they believe she decided to fight back because she knew my wife and I were going to need her support to help get us through my health crisis. Only she could confirm that, and if it's true, I can honestly say it was the most caring, beautiful, and unselfish act anyone has ever done for me and my family, and I could never thank her enough. Her fight for life not only gave me hope, but made me appreciate life like never before.

Coming of Age
Sheila Buska

I was sure I'd live to be a hundred with not a health problem in sight. I stayed away from doctors—they were for sick people. I figured I'd die in my sleep after finishing off a hot fudge sundae and enjoying an evening with my children and grandchildren—all this of course, after a busy day at the office.

Suddenly I'm minus a few body parts—no longer essential, thank goodness—and under constant surveillance by doctors and machines. The word cancer has entered my vocabulary.

They said they got it all, that it was a particularly stubborn type. Not a surprise, since I can't count the number of times my mother took me aside to point out the pluses and minuses of being stubborn. This stubborn cancer landed in my womb, so—off with the womb!

Coming to after surgery, I felt like I'd been through World War II. Delivering four babies in five years, having a childhood tonsillectomy, and twenty years of driving in the fast lane of the California freeways never prepared me for this. Three days later the doctor walked in and told me I could go home. *Go home?! I could barely move.* I'd eaten the grand total of four slurps of orange sherbet and six sips of apple juice since the surgery.

Going home was the best thing I ever did. The first morning I gave myself a sponge bath, weakly patting various parts of my body with a warm, soapy washcloth. The second morning I poured cupfuls of water over my head, rubbed in some shampoo and voila, clean hair! I still couldn't eat much; everything tasted funny—metallic funny.

The third morning I put on clothes that used to be too big. Now my huge pooch stuck out where my not-so-flat tummy used to be. How can they take out all that stuff and you end up with a balloon stomach—looking six months' pregnant?

This is reality now, no more head in the sand. I had cancer to fight. A call had come in from the hematology/oncology department. Scheduled for an appointment on Monday, only four days away, I wondered how I'd walk from the parking lot to the fourth floor of the medical office. I told myself not to worry. *I'll reschedule the appointment. Go later in the week. Besides, I need time to think about this cancer thing.*

At home, life got better as I walked around the house every hour or so. Lots of baseball division playoffs to watch on TV helped, but not as much as the prayers and well wishes of friends and family—and the candy from Dad.

The day before the appointment, I stepped outside. Blue sky, birds singing, new lavender buds on the chrysanthemums. Fantastic!

The next day I gathered my meager strength and dialed the hematology/oncology number. As I waited, a small voice suggested, *Why not just go? Find out about this treatment plan.*

Time to grow up, cancer is cancer and doctors would become my friends and a fact of life for me, like it or not. Besides, the fight in me had surfaced. I was ready for the first round. I'd be at that appointment if someone had to bring me in a wheelchair. I was a stubborn cuss, so yes, I made it. Looked like an ol' lady of ninety-seven, shuffling down those long corridors in my unzipped slacks covered over with a generous size sweater, but I made it.

The hematologist/oncologist said the surgeon got all the cancer out and none was found in the twenty-nine lymph nodes the surgeon helped himself to, *but*... he still recommended radiation therapy. No chemotherapy—I let out a sigh of relief. At home I made the appointment and eased myself down onto the couch. *Ahhhh... two free days before Staple Removal Day.* I hadn't counted them, unable to see them below the equator of my waistline, but I knew there were over twenty. Only two of them really got me, thus I survived staple removal.

At my post-op checkup, the doctor said my remaining parts were in unusually excellent condition. This led me to question the benefits of attacking these healthy parts with large doses of radiation. I explored the American Cancer Society and National Cancer Institute websites to learn more about my particular brand of cancer and the various treatments. Information on these sites encouraged me to dream of the possibility of needing no radiation.

When the call came, I was getting a haircut. I had recovered my ability to eat, walk, and dress sort of normally, but not enough to leap out of the chair and race across the room to answer my phone. The radiation therapist had spoken with the surgeon and was ready to talk to me about treatment and asked me to call her back.

I dreaded calling. I'd been leaning toward the no-radiation treatment, and I was about to hear the decision of two highly respected doctors. Sure they'd recommend radiation, I paid for my haircut, went to my car, and drove to a familiar parking lot where I said a prayer, sucked in my breath, and made the call.

If you happened to be in that parking lot and saw a lady shoot straight up and out the moon-roof of a gray sedan, yelling happy cheers—that was me.

"Your doctor recommends no further treatment."

I was lucky. I think of all the people who are not so fortunate, and I admire them for their bravery and perseverance; I pray for them and wish them wellness soon. And I thank all the people who prayed for me and supported me. I exercise, eat lots of broccoli, carrots, fresh fruit, and whole grains. I wish the best of health and happiness to all.

Nurturing Nurses

Brenda Elsagher

My friend Bob had been in and out of the hospital as diabetes chipped away at Bob's body. His wife, Marge, was constantly by his side. The nursing staff always liked to be with them because they were lots of fun and Bob was a kind patient. On one particular occasion, Bob was acting kind of down and no one was used to that; he wasn't typically a complainer. The nurses teased him out of the situation. They told him they needed to lift him up so they planned a wine and cheese party for the afternoon.

At the designated time, a few nurses came into Bob's room with some string cheese. "Are you ready for the wine?" a nurse asked.

"Sure," replied Bob. He always liked a party.

The nurses gathered together and began to whine. "I don't want to be here," "I'm tired," "My feet hurt," "I want to go home."

Then everybody laughed and Bob and Marge smiled long after the party ended.

Nurses are an essential part of a patient's well-being. They are often compassionate listeners as well as educators for patients. Often they are our cheerleaders for our daily accomplishments back to health. They are highly educated and can enjoy a good laugh at work once in awhile and often at their own expense, as you'll read in the following stories.

Negative Concerns
Kathy Fritz

When I first started working at Fairview Clinic in Burnsville, Minnesota, we used to go out in the lobby and call the patient's name. When they came up to the desk we would tell them the results of their throat culture.

One day I picked up a slip and quickly read that it was negative, so I called the patient in the lobby and told her that her culture was negative and that she should gargle with warm salt water and that it would get better in a few days. She looked at me strangely and said, "What? I just had a pregnancy test. I don't think gargling will help the situation."

We both had a few laughs from that one. I found it helps to read the whole lab slip before calling anyone now.

Clean Up Duty
Shirley Stille

In the 1970s, I was working evenings with an old licensed practical nurse (LPN) and a new aide in a small rural hospital on the medical/surgical floor. We had a sweet, little, old man with dementia in the ward. Because the man was incontinent, the old LPN told the young aide, "Go in, turn the man, and place the urinal."

After what seemed like a long time for the aide to be occupied with the patient, she came out and announced she needed help. We quickly followed her into the room.

"Well, I just can't get this urinal placed," she said exasperated.

We both looked at each other wondering why it would be hard to put the patient's penis in a urinal. Upon uncovering the patient we realized the problem. She was trying to fit *everything* into the urinal and that would have been impossible. Even though the patient was demented, we tried hard not to laugh; there were other patients in the room too. We quietly showed the aide what placing the urinal meant. By the time we got out into the hall, we were silently laughing so hard that the old LPN had a plumbing leak down her legs, into her shoes, and on to the floor.

She gasped, and, of course, the quiet laughing only increased the problem. Another gush happened as we went down the hall toward the bathroom. Instead of cleaning up after the patients, we had to clean up ourselves!

Flossie

Christina Cahall

Flossie was tall, slim, had a creamy complexion and wore her chocolate brown hair pulled back into an elegant chignon. Her hair was set off by a starched uniform and a crisp, white nurse's cap. Intimidated by her exotic blend of glamour and stern, professional demeanor, I failed to notice the twinkle in her snappy, brown eyes. I was anxious in my new assignment as an aide on the medical unit.

This was twenty-two-year-old Flossie's first job as an RN, but she had the aura and skills of a more seasoned nurse. Her name was Ileana, but staff, doctors, even the patients, called her Flossie. I had never met anyone like her. The first two weeks of work were dreadful. She teased me endlessly, and I thought that Flossie was rude and brassy. She delighted in embarrassing me once she found out how easy it was to make me blush. No topic was too sacred for Flossie to make fun of or ridicule. I'd rarely been around a woman who talked in such a blunt and open way. I couldn't understand why the doctors, nurses, and patients enjoyed her teasing manners, but I had to admit that on her days off, the hours crept by and could be boring.

Flossie loved practical jokes and one day told me to get a urine specimen marked "Mrs. Apple" out of the refrigerator. Back then we used six-ounce, sterilized, thick glass containers. This one was filled to the brim with the familiar amber-colored liquid. I handed the specimen to Flossie. She removed the lid, chugged the contents, and smacked her lips as though she enjoyed every drop. We gasped as she bent over with laughter. She went to the ward refrigerator and showed us a jug of cider that she'd brought in for the staff.

One of our favorite patients, Marie, seldom complained, and appreciated the care we gave her. Not permitted to look at the charts, I wasn't sure what was wrong with Marie. Someone whispered that she had uremia and that it was usually fatal. This was back in 1953, before dialysis had become a routine treatment. Marie had a crisis one night. We were short-staffed and Flossie asked me to help her with Marie. Marie had no family, so the two of us stayed with her. We changed her sheets, bathed her, wiped the perspiration from her frail body, and massaged her back, doing our best to make her comfortable.

I saw another side of Flossie—she was a good, caring nurse. After a couple of hours, Flossie made me leave, even though I begged to stay. I know she was protecting me from seeing Marie's death. When she died that night, she wasn't alone, because Flossie never left her side.

Later, Flossie encouraged me to attend nursing school, and I was the proud recipient of a scholarship from the same school she had attended. She gave me a party when I resigned to go off to nursing school, and her antics with patients and staff continued. My mother used to say, "Don't be too quick to judge someone." It took Flossie to show me the value of that good advice.

Mistaken Identity
Joan Clayton

During World War II, doctors were scarce. In our small town, Dr. Swisher worked long hours with packed patients who filled the reception room. When one attended patient left, the nurse called out the next ones by their last names.

She called out the name, "Smiths" and a couple got up and followed her. The nurse took them to the examining room and pulled the curtain around the table. The doctor came in and gave the woman a pelvic examination. He came from behind the curtain and proceeded to tell the man his diagnosis of Mrs. Smith.

"But Doctor Swisher," the man said, "I never saw this woman before in my life!"

The man and woman just happened to have the same last name and were sitting next to each other in the reception room.

The Gospel According to Ruth Ann
Hope Sunderland

My daydream vanished as Ruth Ann bounded through the recovery room doors and headed straight for me. I groaned and stood straighter, the bedside rails I'd propped myself against clanging. I'd been caught paying less-than-rapt attention to my patient, and the stark decor of the anti-septic recovery room left nowhere to hide. Only moments before, when the patient arrived from surgery, I'd checked his vital signs and airway before my attention drifted.

Our nursing class was graduating in a few short weeks, and senioritis raged. I had an acute case and hadn't considered it could be fatal. But the look in Ruth Ann's eyes told me I was wrong.

As Mrs. Francis, the instructor I most feared, approached, I got the feeling in the pit of my stomach that a traffic cop's flashing red light in my rearview mirror caused. As she zeroed in, I fiddled with the blood pressure cuff, hoping to avert the likely questions. Ruth Ann, as her name implied, could be ruthless when it came to queries. The only rubber hose I ever saw her with was on the end of an enema bucket, but should inquisition become an Olympic event, Ruth Ann was a world-class competitor.

"Miss Sunderland," she crooned, emphasizing the "Miss" a little too much. I felt like she was the early bird and I was the worm.

"Do you notice anything unusual about your patient?"

"Well—no."

"Maybe you should note his respirations and his color."

So with great flair, I watched the second hand tick on my watch and counted the man's respirations for sixty seconds. I'd been taught to take vital signs for a full minute, but quickly fell into the fifteen-seconds-times-four habit. Had judges observed, I'd have scored perfect tens for artistic impression.

After an exhaustive minute, I reported that his respirations were, "Three."

"His color?"

"Blue!"

Ruth Ann then suggested with remarkable self-control, that I report those findings to the recovery room supervisor. Fortunately, the head nurse had already noted the problem and notified the anesthesiologist. The patient, immediately treated, recovered in a few moments. It took me much longer.

My instructor raised her eyebrows slightly and her silence thundered. As the gravity of my error sank in, I vowed to pay attention. Ruth Ann distributed guilt like she owned the franchise.

I had not always called her Ruth Ann and certainly never to her face. When she taught sociology my freshman year, she initially terrified me.

Her face was pleasantly rounded, as was the rest of her. And she sported a rosy cast to her cheeks and the tip of her nose, looking like a refugee from a winter storm. I mused that she'd make a perfect shopping mall Mrs. Santa. Her eyes crinkled warmly when she smiled, which she did not often do. Underneath the starched nursing cap, her thinning hair was peppered with gray and defied a true hairstyle. She never looked quite neat, something I identified with.

Sociology bored me, especially references involving "upper upper." To this unsophisticated, small town girl, classes were foreign, found in distant places like India. In the margin of my book, I doodled cartoons of Ruth Ann wearing a sari.

She taught me gems of wisdom such as "Animals are raised, children are reared," delivering that pearl in red ink in the margin of a term paper. Exclamation point! Exclamation point! Exclamation point!

In the late 1960s school of nursing, when I advanced from the classroom to practical experience, Ruth Ann was frequently assigned as my clinical instructor. Her presence tied knots in my stomach. By the time we studied colitis, I was too familiar with the symptoms.

My initial clinical experience came after weeks of practice bed baths on other students. Anxiety gripped me when my patient needed not only a bath, but an enema. It might as well have been brain surgery. I wasn't sure if I dreaded the enema or Ruth Ann's watchful eye more. With her help, I survived both the soap suds and the nerves. And so did the patient.

Ruth Ann's questions could be brutal, and I thought my blue-and-white striped student pinafore drew her like a red cape taunts a charging bull. I never dodged her surveillance and suspected a small blipping radar antenna lurked under her cap, tracking my location.

Always, she expected me to know too much. When I couldn't respond to a question, she smiled sweetly and suggested, "Well, why don't you look that up tonight?"

Sometimes that required long hours in the library, and once I knew the answer, she rarely asked again. After I'd researched central venous pressures and was a walking genius on the subject, the least she could do was let me show off. But the next inquisition would target aortic grafts and why they leaked. And back to the textbooks I'd go. I lost track of canceled plans. Ruth Ann didn't care if Ben Casey needed me.

Eventually, I wearied of dodging her and determined that I would outwit her. This was war. I'd learn everything before she asked. So I studied in earnest and anticipated her probing. And though I saw the smile crinkles around her eyes more often, she always had a zinger up her starched uniform sleeve. I studied harder. As a side effect, my grades improved, and I read sometimes because a subject was fascinating, not because it was required. Alas, I learned.

I grew to respect Ruth Ann. But for one thing, I thought I would never forgive her.

Before graduation, she discovered that I lacked orthopedic experience. Consequently, she remedied my educational shortfall with a patient sporting a hip-spica cast. The middle-aged woman was morbidly obese, and I found her crude and repulsive. By her own account, she had fallen off her front porch while dead drunk, causing her complicated fracture. She cackled loudly through a snaggled smile, throwing her head back as dark, greasy hair fell in clumps around her rotund face. And could she swear. I developed an immediate dislike for her, as had everyone else on the unit.

When I stopped by her room to introduce myself, an after shave commercial played on the overhead television. A sleepy, early-rising, freshly-shaved guy loudly slapped himself awake with a fragrant bracing tingle, declaring, "Thanks. I needed that!" I took it as an omen and left the room muttering, "Thanks, Ruth Ann. I didn't need this!"

I thought "the hip-spica" relished attention a little too much, and though her restrictive cast severely limited her independence, I resented giving her needed assistance. I gritted my teeth daily when I arrived to help with her morning routine. And the needle on my compassion meter stayed stuck on "EMPTY."

Her bathing ritual included potent cologne, her prized possession and a gift from her daughter, who lived in another state. After she doused herself in honeysuckle, she reeked like the vines themselves after a downpour. She insisted on sharing, until I learned to stay out of dabbing range.

As the weeks wore on, she never had visitors. With graduation a few days away and my own marriage approaching, I was lost in my future and neglected to prepare her for my departure. When I explained that I was leaving, she surveyed me strangely for a long moment. Then her lower lip quivered and she started bawling loudly. "But who'll take care of me now?" she sobbed.

Too embarrassed to comfort her and already late to class, I tried to make my exit.

Snuffling loudly, she thanked me and strained to reach for her honey-suckle cologne. I refused when she tried to give it to me, but was touched by the gesture. She was hurt until I explained that students were strictly forbidden to accept gifts. Satisfied, she perched the cologne back on the nightstand and dabbed her eyes with tissue. I couldn't speak for the lump in my throat, so I departed with a shake of my head and an awkward wave.

Tears of shame stung my eyes as I bumped into Ruth Ann. She noted the tears and this time, it was I who asked the question.

As students, our primary focus was learning, not labor. Consequently, our patients usually received superior care. I asked Mrs. Francis to see that another student was assigned to my patient during the rest of her stay. Ruth Ann nodded her approval.

And as I sauntered off the hospital floor for the last time as a student nurse, I whispered softly to myself, "Thanks, Ruth Ann. I needed that!"

Paging Faux Pas

Dan Tyrrell

Recently, I had abominable abdominal surgery at Cleveland Clinic. My nurse for the day was a fine gentleman named Lou. This was his last shift of three, twelve-hour days. While attending to my needs, he received a page, "Lou, the ET (enterstomal nurse) wants to see you in bed nine immediately."

He left right away amid a chorus of laughter. When he returned, he was as red as a beet.

Patients are a Gift

Shirley Stille

I took care of a wonderful lady after she had surgery to remove her bladder due to cancer, leaving her with a permanent urostomy. She was very anxious, scared about her diagnosis, and feeling overwhelmed with everything. She was a nervous mess, near to tears, and kept saying, "I will never be able to handle this."

I let her vent, gave her a hug, and said, "You will be a pro in six months, I promise. It will be like brushing your teeth."

She said, "Never!"

I worked with this lady very patiently, and with each visit she settled down more and more. Her poor hands shook, she was easily frustrated because she had no control of the urine, and it would just keep coming. I showed her all the tricks, how to stay dry and still change the appliance. She always called when things went wrong or when they went right, and I always responded with support and praise. It's been over a year since her surgery and she now laughs at how she was in the beginning. She always has the biggest hug and kiss for me because at six months she was a pro. I still get updates, and then I get another chance to tell her how well she is doing.

She recently developed a peristomal hernia and we had to fit her with a support belt and she never blinked an eye. This is why I do what I do, to see the patient independent, happy, and living life to its fullest. I feel humbled to be a part of this process with my patients. They let me into their lives, which helps me to grow in mine. I can't imagine doing any other type of nursing anymore, I want to see, interact, and build relationships with my patients. Sometimes the outcomes aren't always great, but I am there for them and they for me—it's an amazing connection unlike any other time in my thirty-five years of nursing.

Lay people don't usually think like a health care professional. We must always put the patient and their family first and foremost—with understandable and complete explanations. Every time I have had the unfortunate pleasure of experiencing something medical done to myself, I realize more how patients feel. Those experiences grow me as a nurse and I am all the better for my patients.

No Gas Shortages
Midge Willson

In my former job as a wound, ostomy, and continent nurse in acute care, I heard stories that reflected the humor of a bad situation.

One patient was having a terrible time dealing with ulcerative colitis, which resulted in frequent trots and noisy gas. One morning she was in the bathroom exploding away when her seven-year-old son knocked on the door, "Are you moving furniture in there?"

Another fellow experiencing a lot of post op gas said, "Those are some real blanket raisers."

The Evil Nurse
Richard Lewis

The morning I went to the hospital for an operation to remove my gallbladder, I expected to be leaving by noon. Instead, I had a problem with the anesthesia and I was kept overnight for observation. A large clock hung on the wall at the foot of my bed, each hour a nurse would enter, awaken me, and ask me the time and date. Next, she'd ask if I needed to go to the bathroom, and after I declined, she would give me a pill and leave.

The nurse on the evening shift was most unfriendly and sometimes she could hardly waken me.

Rubbing my eyes to see the clock, I'd reply, "6:10 on December 15, 7:10 on December 15," etc. and "No, I don't need the bathroom."

As each hour passed, the nurse became more insistent that I go to the bathroom and offered me a bedpan, but each time I failed to deliver. As the evening progressed she became more irritated with me as sometimes it was difficult to wake me up, but I would try to be friendly as I began to fear her visits.

Upon being awakened at 12:10 a.m., I replied, "It's 12:10 of December 15."

She wickedly smiled for the first time and said, "You are wrong, it is December 16."

I quickly replied, "That's a trick question, it's only been December 16 for ten minutes."

She refused to accept my defense.

I told her, "December 15 has been on my mind and my calendar for weeks as I waited for this operation; naturally I was still thinking it was the 15th."

As I protested, she grew more upset with me when I could not use the bedpan.

"If you still can't use it in the next hour, I'll be forced to use a catheter."

"What does that mean?" I asked.

She smiled broadly and rudely replied, "I'd shove a tube up your penis to your bladder and drain you." She then left the room while I lay in a state of fear.

I drifted in and out of sleep for the next hour but mostly broke out in a cold sweat thinking about what she said. I was awake and waiting for her at 1:10 and gave her the correct answer of December 16. She then happily handed me the bedpan and with a great deal of difficulty, I was able to make a small deposit. The nurse seemed visibly disappointed as she removed the bedpan.

Then, handing me another pill, she said, "You're lucky it worked."

Everything's Coming Up Posey

Marilyn Ashenbrener

Patient safety is the number one concern of any hospital or nursing home. Over the years, ideas of what to do to keep patients safe with impaired judgment or perhaps an unstable gait have grown and changed. In the 1980s, the use of a Posey vest was one way to prevent patients from harm. The vest was made of a mesh material and had two long ties that could be tied to the bed frame to prevent a person from getting out of bed. Yet, at the same time, the vest was designed in such a way so it was least restrictive in that the patient could easily turn side to side or sit up while in bed.

The plan was the patients would realize when trying to get out of bed that the vest was preventing them from doing so and, therefore, they would remember they needed to call for help. Also, frequent checks by nursing personnel were made. More than once, a wearer of such a safety device had kindly asked me for a scissors to cut off the strap to the jacket, not understanding it was on for their safety.

I won't forget one night when I worked at a nursing home that a client there was known to have "sundowners" syndrome—confused mostly at night. For her safety, she wore a Posey jacket at night. But one night upon making rounds, the nursing assistant did not find her in her bed. After quickly checking the room, she called for help and had all the staff looking for this sweet lady. About to start looking for her outside, someone found her safely in her bed! After making sure she was okay, the nurse asked if she was indeed out of her bed, or if some mistake was made by the nursing assistant. The lady said, oh, yes, she went to the bathroom down the hall. And she did just fine, but she had the hardest time getting back into her Posey jacket!

Joe
Pamela Goldstein

I used to work nights in the ER. During one shift, the police brought in the most serene autoworker with a beatific smile on his face. They caught him smashing windows of houses while he shouted threats to the "whores" who lived there.

As I filled out admission papers, Joe talked amiably to the air in our psychiatric room. He chortled, "That's a good one!"

"Who's he talking to?" I asked.

"Jesus," said the cop. "They're best buddies." He nodded toward the man. "Careful. His co-workers said he just suddenly went berserk."

I knocked on the door of the room. "Hi, Joe," I said. "May I come in?"

"Sure, hon. We're just shootin' the s--t."

He looked lovingly at the space next to him. "Sure, sure," he said to the air. "You go on ahead while I talk to the nurse." He winked at me. "You're wondering what happened tonight."

"Yes, I am," I replied.

"It was the most amazing thing. My wife left me and took our kids. I crashed my car and the roof on the house caved in. So I'm working on the fender line, feeling mighty sorry for myself, when all of a sudden Jesus came walking down the line. He was as magnificent as I always dreamed he'd be. And then he stopped right in front of me! He said, 'Joe, it's time for you to stop working here. I need you to do the Lord's work. You have to clear out all of the whores in this town. I'll show you where they live.'"

Joe suddenly nodded his head and laughed. "Yeah, okay, man. I'll tell her." He grinned. "Jesus wants you to know we was both hungry, so we stopped at Burger King before getting started." He laughed even more. "Yeah, me too!"

"What did he say?" I asked, then grimaced for asking. We weren't supposed to acknowledge hallucinations.

"He says he always gets the squirts after eating at the BK."

Joe frowned. "No, just because she's got big boobs don't mean she's a whore. She's a nurse, very innocent looking." He looked at me. "He thinks you're a whore because of your boobs. Women didn't have boobs like that in his day."

I blushed. "It's the way I'm built."

Joe shrugged. "I don't know, man. Ask her yourself."

"What?" I asked.

"Jesus wants to know what you're doing after work. He and I are going to the bar across the street for a few brewskies."

I cleared my throat. "I'm busy."

Joe continued to tell me about the night, stopping every few minutes to laugh at something his pal said.

"Joe, I don't see Jesus," I said. "He's here?"

"That's a real shame, sweetheart, because he is beautiful." He leaned forward. "And he's a helluva good joke teller. Raunchy, though."

"So he's in this room?"

"Oh, yeah, yeah, for sure," said Joe. He pointed toward the bathroom. "He's on the toilet, taking a dump."

The other staff howled with laughter when I looked in the bathroom to see. We admitted Joe to the psychiatric unit. Several days later I saw Joe in the coffee shop of the hospital. He looked dejected, disconsolate–lonely.

"May I join you, Joe?" I asked.

Joe nodded.

"How are you doing?"

"He disappeared."

"You mean Jesus?"

Joe sighed. "The Doc says I was delusional because of all the crap that happened to me. But Jesus seemed so real. I felt so happy with him around, like I had the strength to do anything. Now he's gone." Joe held up a Bible. "Doc gave me this. He says Jesus is here."

Joe patted my hand. "I guess you don't understand, being you're Jewish and all."

"I understand, Joe. Jews have always needed God's strength."

I took the Bible and thumbed through it. "You ever read the Bible, Joe?"

"No."

I read several Psalms to him, the joyful ones. "What do you think?"

"Who wrote that?"

"King David. He loved God. And his life was no bed of roses, believe me."

Joe took the Bible from me. "I gotta go," he said.

I didn't see Joe during the rest of his stay, and after a while, I forgot about him. Several years passed and one day he found me at the hospital. A woman was with him.

"Hey, do you remember me?"

I shook my head. "No, Reverend, I'm sorry."

"It's me, Joe, the crazy guy. You read me Psalms when I was really down."

"Ohhhh, I remember you now," I said. "Joe."

"Yeah, yeah, I knew you would. You seemed like the type. I went back to my room that day and read the Bible. I fell in love with it and King David became my hero. So, after I left the hospital, I went into the seminary and became a minister." He tugged on the woman next to him. "This is my new wife, Susan. We're on our way to South America. I've got a congregation to lead."

"That's wonderful, Joe."

"Yeah, I'm very happy." He embraced me. "I just wanted you to know that I'm okay, now. I never knew your name, but I never forgot you. You know how God sends us angels when we're in need? He sent me you. Thanks."

He turned to leave and then stopped. "I always wondered though. Out of all the guardian angels, why did God send me a Jewish one? And then I figured it out. King David was Jewish!"

I laughed. "I've got news for you, Joe. So was Jesus."

Tender Times

Brenda Elsagher

I was pounding the keys one day when the phone rang. "Hello, this is Brenda," I answered.

"My name is Teresa. I just finished reading your book, *If the Battle is Over, Why am I Still in Uniform?* I could really relate to it. I was diagnosed with colorectal cancer, too. I was wondering if you would have the time to come to our local cancer support group and give a talk."

It turned out Teresa lived near me, just a couple of miles away, and the cancer support group was held at a church not far from me. As she talked further, I realized we did have a lot in common except that she was diagnosed with stage 4 colorectal cancer, and she was fighting for her life. She, like me, had her plumbing rearranged, although she faced a more daunting task ahead with many rounds of chemotherapy, hoping against odds that she would go into remission. She was a forty-three-year-old woman with three school age children and a good husband. She had just run a 5K race and was feeling pretty good when she was shocked to learn she was in the advanced stages of colon cancer.

I agreed to give a talk to the support group and later Teresa and I had lunch together. We also talked on the phone once or twice. I liked her. We laughed and teased each other like we'd known one another for years.

A couple of months later, I was driving by her neighborhood. On a whim, I called her. "Hi, Teresa, you're still alive!" We both laughed. "It's good to hear your voice. By chance can you get away to have a margarita and some chips. I'm in your area."

From earlier conversations, we discovered we both liked a favorite local Mexican restaurant. "I am so up for that!" was her response. Shortly after, I picked her up and two hours flew by, well spent in the company of a soul sister.

Months went by again and in November we ran into each other at my church bazaar and caught up over cinnamon rolls and hot chocolate. The chemo hadn't worked so far but she was still trying new treatments. Teresa told me about some trips she had taken and the special days with her kids each month where she let them skip school to hang out with her. A famous one for scrapbooking, she was always urging me to come over to her house and scrap with her. I never seemed to find the time or the desire for that.

In January, I got a call from Teresa with some bad news. "Brenda, I found out today that the cancer has spread to my brain. My time is running out, and I want to start planning my funeral. I wondered if you would do my eulogy."

"Sure, Teresa," I stammered. Then I teased her a little. "Are you sure you have given this enough thought? I think the cancer has gotten to your brain all right, we hardly know each other. I don't know your kids or your husband; I've never been in your house. Don't you think a family member or long-time friend would be more appropriate?"

"No, I want you, Brenda. I want my eulogy to be funny, and I want you to give everyone a parting gift from me—to remind them to get their colonoscopies."

"Teresa, I'd feel better if I came over to your house, got to know your husband, your kids, and even you better. Then if everyone agrees and you don't change your mind, I'll be happy to do it."

That began a series of visits with Teresa and her husband at their home. I saw her obsession with scrapbooking and she was good at it. Her husband designed a room for her and she was surrounded by all the things she needed to make her beautiful pages or framed artwork. I saw how she interacted with her children, heard her life stories, and we talked frankly about the days ahead.

Three days before she died, I went to visit her for the last time. I was going out of town to speak the next day, and I wanted to check up on her. She had been in and out of a deep sleep and I remember her waking up, looking me in the eyes, and asking, "Have I done enough?"

"Yes, Teresa, you've done enough—including scrapbooking everything that walked by."

At her funeral, I felt like I walked into a room of three hundred strangers. We didn't have friends in common, and I had only gotten to know a handful of her family members and friends in my visits over the prior few months. It was an honor to deliver her eulogy—it felt like one of the most important talks I would ever give in my life. I wanted it to be special for her husband and children.

The crowd laughed as they remembered her antics and it was a true celebration of her life and love. Each person walked away with the parting gift Teresa had requested. When it was over, I was embraced by her family and friends, and walked out with a few hundred new friends through Teresa. Two months later, I made my first scrapbook and thought of her with each page. Since then, I've thought of Teresa many times and continued to make scrapbooks for my family.

We are impacted by the people we love. Some come into our lives for just a few months while others are known to us for years. The following stories show the range of love and humor in the difficult times and how they often go hand in hand.

Valentine Dinner and the Hoist

Lori La Bey

I remember Valentine's dinner at Red Lobster the year after my dad passed away. My mother, Dorothy, looked beautiful. Her hair was perfect, her perfume filled the air, and she was wearing red, her favorite color. Mom boasted to all at dinner about her spa day at the VOA, code to the rest of us: nursing home. She bragged about doing her own nails, which we knew Chris the beautician, or Bobbie in activities did for her, but it really did not matter. Mom looked great and felt wonderful.

During dinner with eyes glistening, a broad smile, and pride beaming, Mother proceeded to tell us how the staff hoisted her above the whirlpool and lowered her gently in to soak. You could see her mind melt as she told of the caressing jets pumping lightly against her body.

I visualized a crane-like machine lifting my mother, a large woman of 280 pounds into a whirlpool tub. I bit my cheeks to stop from laughing and noticed the rest of the family doing the same. For us, this was no relaxing spa-like treatment, but to my mother it was heavenly. The peace and calmness lit up her face and impressed us all. At that moment, we all wanted a little of what she had experienced.

Mom was actually trying to make us all jealous of her luxurious life. It was fantastic how much she loved her home, her resort. In this stage of Alzheimer's disease, Mother could sometimes still grasp the big picture and connect the dots. She understood her arthritis made it difficult for her to get in and out of the tub and the hoist allowed her the experience where she could sit, soak, and enjoy. What her mind chooses to hold onto at times amazes me.

A Husband's Tender Touch
Renee Rongen

As I walked in the back door of my husband's parents' house, I stepped over familiar untied tennis shoes and work boots before landing in the kitchen long enough to set the latest medical bills on the counter next to the bin of Loracet, Prednisone, and Tylox bottles. I headed down the hall where my mother-in-law lay in a hospital bed in what had previously been her sewing room. Hearing the harsh sound of bed rails as they dropped down from their upright position, I hurried towards the room, afraid that something had happened, when I heard giggling. I stopped and listened wondering who was tending to my mother-in-law? I saw the full-time nurse charting in a nearby office, so I took another step closer and put my ear to the half-cracked open door. That laugh I definitely recognized; it was my husband's. I was about to step in and announce my presence when I heard my husband say to his mother, "Mom, this ain't nothing, at least you don't squirm around and throw your legs over your head like Elizabeth." Elizabeth was our two-year-old and my husband was describing her routine diaper change.

I listened further as my husband and his mother conferred about the tightness of her adult diaper he was changing.

He laughed as he asked her, "Mom, do you want a firm, snug fit, or do you think you want the less bound, loose fit?"

She laughed and, in what had become over time her quiet voice, replied with her hint of humor, "Oh, you better give me the firm and snug fit. You never know when I am going to bound out of this bed and begin my callisthenic routine."

I smiled and almost broke into laughter, as it was a familiar bantering of words and wit between the two of them. It was their way of masking the unbearable truth of what had become of his fifty-eight-year-old mother. A vibrant, beautiful woman now lying on a hospital bed, head wrapped in a crooked yellow and black turban, eyes sunken in, and a new body that was twice her size brought on with daily doses of prednisone and other cancer cocktail drugs.

I leaned in closer as the silence penetrated the room. Thinking his mother was worn out by all of the activity of changing her adult garb, I was about to step into the room again. Just as my left foot began to tiptoe in, I heard my mother-in-law say to my husband, her son, "You are such a gift to me. You make me laugh when I should be red with embarrassment. Son, I am so proud of the man you have become. You are a great father and wonderful husband. You know, your father would have been so proud of you. Thank you for taking such good care of me." In the next breath, her voice was almost a faint whisper and she said; "Let's pray." She began, "God, I am so thankful for this day and for this moment to be alive. Thank you for the laughter and for the gift of my son today. I know all things are possible through you and I ask that you use me in such a way as to glorify your name."

Together I heard them whisper through their sniffles, "Amen."

I opened the door slowly just in time to see my husband's lips gently lay a kiss on the woman who gave him life and encouraged him to live his own.

"I love you, Mom," he whispered in her ear.

Her eyes now shut, she mouthed the words back, "I know."

More Than Simply Arthritis
Shirley Cheng

"A...ar...art..." Juliet Cheng muttered, running her finger down her red English-Chinese dictionary and stopping when it reached its destination—arthritis. She read the definition of the name the doctor had just recently labeled her baby daughter.

Arthritis? I know many people who have it, so it does not seem so serious.

The previous doctor told Juliet there was nothing wrong with her baby. At first, it comforted Juliet. But quickly that comfort turned into discomfort. If nothing was wrong with her daughter, then why was she screaming in agony? Why would her tiny body shake whenever Juliet applied even the slightest pressure on her daughter's legs? And why were her joints red and swollen? No, there must be something the matter with her, and now Juliet knew that something was arthritis. Tests results confirmed by the doctor told her that her daughter, Shirley, had juvenile rheumatoid arthritis.

Once back home from the hospital, Juliet consulted one of her trusty books, the Chinese medical dictionary, which listed many of the diseases accompanied by photographs that were anything but pleasing to the eye. After days of fruitless guessing, worrying, and searching, as Juliet read the symptoms of this particular arthritis and found there was no cure, her heart sank.

A few days earlier Shirley cried uncontrollably when Juliet gently touched her. Shirley had developed a high fever, followed by swollen joints just five days after receiving a tuberculin skin test. *Who could have thought that a tuberculin skin test could have such a horrifying outcome?* thought Juliet.

It could cripple my pearl, thought Juliet when that possibility hit her. However, as soon as that negative thought sprang into mind, she quickly washed it away. She salvaged the pieces of her painful heart and thought, *Let that disease try to win and fail.* Then and there, she vowed, *I am going to use everything I have and anything the world has to offer to make life the best experience for Shirley.* She would see to it that Shirley would be the prettiest princess on a wheelchair the world had ever seen. The disease could only touch her body; with Jehovah God's help, Juliet would make sure it would never touch her soul. She knew she would stand by her daughter's side at all costs. If she had to carry her over high mountains or rescue her from the depths of the oceans, she would. And if she had to set her aims high to reach a star or two, she would, and if it had to take everything for her to be a successful mother, then let it be so, for Shirley was more than the world to her.

Many challenges awaited both Juliet and Shirley; with every defeat, they would graduate to conquer even tougher obstacles. Initially, Shirley's days were spent in constant pain, making daily chores like dressing and bathing highly difficult. Juliet spent nights rocking the suffering baby to sleep, often lasting into the early morning hours. Worn down, Juliet became physically exhausted caring for her baby twenty-four hours a day, seven days a week, who by her thirteenth month of life, was knocking on death's door. The crippling disease had rapidly spread to all of the joints in Shirley's body, causing excruciating pain; like a statue, she was unable to move or sit.

Seeing that American hospitals offered no relief for Shirley, Juliet took her to her native country of China to seek remedies to ease Shirley's suffering, and, hopefully, save her life.

That took Juliet to the second stage of challenges, which consisted of six trips to China within ten years. As Juliet had fervently hoped, Shirley's life was not only saved, but at age four, Shirley experienced one full year of walking after receiving effective Western shots combined with massage therapy. For the first time, Shirley explored a world outside of hospital walls. Fascinated by everything she saw, heard, and touched, Shirley experienced new feelings that came with walking, running, and dancing. Juliet had achieved her primary goal of stabilizing Shirley's health and keeping her happy with her pain now tamed under herbal medicines.

Juliet entered the third stage with a goal to maintain Shirley's well-being in mind, body, and spirit as she pursued an education for the first time in her eleven years. Traveling between the USA and China and the years of hospitalization, Shirley knew only her ABCs, simple English, and very basic math. She had no idea where rain came from or what caused a beautiful rainbow to appear. Being the happy and hopeful girl that Juliet had brought her up to be, her soul was uncontaminated by depression or sadness; it was open to absorb knowledge like crystal clear water flows through a mud-free river—without any hindrance.

After Shirley attended a special education class in elementary school for a total of about 180 days in between going to China and studying, her teacher told Juliet, "Shirley is ready to go to a regular sixth grade class, and she will do very well in it."

This sent Shirley and Juliet off to a new world of different hurdles. Just as Juliet expected, this was much more than simply arthritis. With the great relief of Shirley's life prolonged, there was the heartache that stabbed Juliet when the walking days ended soon after the quality of the shots decreased. There was the injustice when Juliet, while in America, was charged with child abuse and her parental rights removed after she refused unwanted and harmful treatments for her daughter. There was the joy when Shirley entered the mainstream school system with a smile that spoke a thousand words, and there was the pride Juliet held when Shirley scored numerous awards and high grades as an honor student. There was the frustration when they tried to find compassion from apathetic people, and there was the laughter shared when Shirley twirled round and round in her power wheelchair in their cozy living room.

As the years passed, horror struck when Shirley lost her eyesight at age seventeen. With immeasurable happiness, Shirley conquered her blindness to become an award-winning author and motivational speaker. There was a strong love, an inseparable bond formed between this mother-daughter team, cheerleaders to one another. Through their trials and tribulations, two bodies became one spiritually, living in each other's hearts, ever wishing, hoping, praying, and dreaming together. After the many exams, mother and daughter have graduated magna cum laude, and they look forward to attending the next class together so they can discover and embrace what more awaits than simply arthritis.

Waterskiing
Lori La Bey

Today, again, my boat was flipped over. My body absorbed the river of denial's cold, bitter water in the darkness of my mind, heart, and soul. As I punched in the security code to go up the elevator, I could feel stabbing pains in my chest. I pushed button number two. I heard the hum of the elevator as it rose. The door opened. I saw the unit Mom just moved from, her home, where she had been the social butterfly of the unit.

Now, as I walked past all her friends, I again reached up to punch in another security code, to enter her new home, the lowest functioning unit for Alzheimer's patients. I took a deep breath, thinking I need all the oxygen I could get, to help me through this moment, this scheduled boat flip.

I bravely pushed the heavy door open and walked into my mother's new unit. The tile floors shined in the brightly lit hallway. I read the nameplates and made note of the memory boxes or prompts next to each door, along with the beautiful pictures to add that homey affect, as I slowly forced myself to walk down the hall.

I heard my mother's voice. My gait quickened, as I rushed towards the sound of her. She was mad; no, she was downright angry. The sound of her voice led me straight to her room. I read her nameplate to the left of the door. This was it, my mother's new room. I stood in the hallway outside her room and listened to the conversation. Mom was yelling, profanity spewed from her lungs. This alone was a statement to the changes my mother had gone through as the disease progressed. In the past, Mom was always the first to shove a bar of soap in your mouth to clean up your language.

"Dorothy," I heard a female staff say in a calm soothing voice. "Dorothy, we are here to help you. We want to get you up and off the bed and into your wheelchair. It's lunch time, Dorothy." There was a brief pause on the staff's part, but my mother kept swearing.

Another voice, this time a man said, "Dorothy, we need your arms straight and knees bent. Come on, Dorothy, you can do this. We are here to help you do this. Once your knees are bent and your arms are straight, I'm going to push the button and the machine will lift you up, and we can get you into your chair."

Tears welled up in my eyes and all became blurred. I could feel warm water streaming down my cheeks; my nose began to run. I listened, clutching my stomach as pain overtook my body. *Poor Mom,* I thought. *The more disconnected her brain becomes, the more fear she feels.* I stood in the doorway paralyzed, and prayed for help. *Please, dear God, help me. Help my mother. Help the staff. How can I make this better? How can I remove Mom's fear and get her calm and responsive? How can I help her? Please, dear God, there has to be something I can do.*

I gathered my courage, prayed for my body to stop shaking, wiped the tears from my eyes, and pushed the heavy, extra wide, handicap door open. No one heard me come in. Mom was still screaming. The staff repeated their request again.

An instant later, I heard my dad's voice as clear as a bell, "Lori, ask Mom to go water skiing." I could feel his arm wrap around my shoulder, and I felt safe. I felt strong. I could do this.

What? Go water skiing? Dad is dead and talking to me. Wow, I'm really losing it this time, I thought. Then, **BOOM.** It hit me. I wiped the tears from my eyes again, walked towards the bed where Mom was sitting, legs out straight, feet off the floor. She was leaning back. Her spine was about one foot off the bed. She continued to scream and yell, in fear, at the staff.

"Mom," I said, as I approached the end of her bed. "Mom, do you want to go water skiing?" Her head turned briskly towards me. She recognized my voice. Her face melted. A blissful calm came over her, and she smiled vibrantly and her glistening eyes glowed and filled the room.

"Yah, of course, I want to go water skiing!" she said in a strong confident tone. Both staff looked at me, as if I was nuts. I couldn't blame them.

"Okay then, let's go water skiing, Mom. KNEES BENT, ARMS STRAIGHT, HIT IT!" I said as I pointed to the staff to push the button. There was a low hum from the machine, and my mother rose proudly off the bed, and up with ease. The smile on her face was like a beautiful sunrise. Her eyes widened in excitement, and the staff, well, they beamed in awe of the whole scene.

"You go, Dorothy!" one of them said, and my mom winked, as she held tight onto the towrope, and glided, in her mind, around the lake.

Hope-Shaped Wings
Diedrich

The old picnic bench was wobbly—and so was I. My head was spinning even as I sat still. My muscles seemed more like trembling jelly, and I, once more, had to stay behind. My cancer-chemo funk was about to ruin another day—or so I thought.

I worried our annual trip to Lake Superior's North Shore might have to be cancelled. Surprisingly, I found myself there with our little dog, Willie, and my dear husband who worried about my care. The special nurse assigned to me had evidently seen something in my face and had convinced the doctor to delay chemo for one week. I hadn't said a word. Somehow, Nurse Mary knew I needed just a bit of hope that day.

Here I was on my beloved lake, still battling an infection as well as the fuzziness that weeks of treatment brings. An avid hiker, my hikes were now uncertain baby steps from car to cabin, to bench and back. I spent my days in bed, catching only glimpses of that sparkling lake, hearing only muted sounds of crashing waves and seagull cries. My husband would take short hikes with our dog and recount his adventures on returning. I was glad for them, but my vacation was more about withdrawal–retreating as best I could to my cocoon. This second-hand life was about to end. I sat at a picnic bench in an isolated spot, with no one else around.

From a cloudless, sunlit sky, they suddenly came dancing into view. Dozens of fluttering wings descended like a cloud. I felt it was a dream–yet, the brush of wings against my cheek and the soft murmuring all around seemed very real. The many flashing glints of light were almost blinding. The vivid colors took my breath away. These were my much-loved Monarchs—royal in their stained-glass cloaks, graceful as a ballet dancer, powered by wings designed for long, amazing flights. Tiny beings, once just worms, yet created to emerge from cocoons as kings! I had never seen so many at one time. As I stood there, mesmerized, great masses vaulted skyward in an instant, only to descend as quickly, each alighting deftly to pirouette on a waiting flower, then to sip its nectar. I felt as if I was in church—in some cathedral filled with sacred dancers, dressed in brilliant hues, acting out a special rite that was meant just for me. I asked myself, "If these tiny, short-lived creatures, these lilies of the field, have such a life, might I not, too, have some purpose left to me?"

Looking back, I know that hope came back to me that day–God's blessed medicine arriving just in time! My butterfly days had just begun, and they continue to this day.

The Sand Trap
Lori La Bey

I grabbed my five iron from my golf bag, turned, and walked toward my ball. The smell of fresh cut grass filled my nostrils. The stark contrast of the deep, rich, green grass nestled up against the bleached, white sand looked beautiful, yet nothing compared to what my eyes saw next.

My mother, a large woman in her sixties, with short, salt and pepper curly hair, lay on her belly in the sand trap. Her big arms stretched over her head. Each finger towered to the knuckles with diamond rings, one on top of the other, ending in a tip of perfectly applied red polish. Her cupped hands trapped the sand as she pulled her arms down and around, in perfect breaststroke form.

I watched in awe. The sand swooshed loudly in my ears. I could hear each grain of sand scraping against one another as she swam. Her head turned sideways as she took in a breath of air, and then rotated her head back into the sand, slightly raised, to adjust for the texture. The confidence and calmness on my mother's face shone like a beacon of light on a pitch black summer evening. She swam in the warm sand to safety. My mind flashed back about twenty years, remembering my mother had always been a great swimmer, and I saw her old lifeguard was still strong and intact.

My God, how are we going to get her out of there. She really thinks she is in the water. Sadness hit me for a brief moment, and then the humor of the situation touched my heart like no other time in my life. I smiled and laughed as I watched her in amazement. My mother's child-like state of mind was rescuing her. She felt safe and in control in this imagined place, in the water. The faith, belief, and power she appeared to hold in this moment seemed incredible.

"Mom, can I help you up?" I asked, as I continued to watch. She abruptly stopped swimming. Her face looked confused as I brought her back to reality. We were golfing. She had fallen in a sand trap.

"Are you ok? Let me help you up," I said in a soft voice accompanied with a warm, friendly smile. She seemed to connect with both immediately, and smiled back at me.

"Ok, Lori. That would be good." Then she burst into laughter, not just a giggle, but a hard solid belly laugh. Her eyes were joyful, yet glistened with tears, and as my mother lay on her stomach in the bleached grains of sand, she seemed to realize for just a second how comical life can be.

The Bank
Jamie Mattes

When I was diagnosed with cancer, my doctors said that I should probably "bank my boys" just in case the chemotherapy would affect me negatively in that area. Off I went to the "bank" and after all of the initial paperwork and screening was completed, I was handed a cup and clipboard. After being instructed about the papers on the clipboard to complete when I was finished, I was escorted to a room.

It was a small area, about half the size of a typical bathroom, furnished with an uncomfortable chair, a small end table with two drawers filled with pornographic magazines and a very small television/VCR. The videos to choose from were in a basket and they were old and had been used many times. This room was not designed by a man because men would have much more comfortable surroundings when doing what needed to be done. There would have been recliners, a couch, maybe some music—you get the gist.

Trying to work on making my deposit, I was not in the mood; besides I couldn't see much on the small screen. The romance was definitely not there so things took a little while. Once the job was done, I labeled the cup and filled out the questionnaire. The whole process was so undignified. I thought the paperwork would be filled with questions like...*did you spill anything? Which hand do you prefer? Did you wash before the job? Did you grunt, groan, or scream while you viewed your video?*

I set my clipboard on the ledge just outside the room and placed the cup of "my boys" on top of it. The lab of this "bank" is in the center of the building, the rooms that we use are around the outside of the lab so the techs watched who came and went; pun intended. As I walked out, the lab tech that was there turned to look at me and gave me a big smile—it kind of freaked me out. I felt like she was saying in her mind—*I know what you just did you naughty, naughty boy.* I raced out of there, glad my deposit was complete.

Going to Heaven in a Body Suit

Renee Rongen

From the cassette player near the hospital bed at my in-laws' home, "The Old Rugged Cross" played softly in the background. I sat curled up in the familiar brown-crocheted afghan across from my sister-in-law. We sat alongside her mother, my dear mother-in-law, who at age fifty-eight was dying far too young from the brain tumors that ravished her body. Lisa and I were more like sisters than in-laws and the woman on the bed was more like a mother to me. We had spent countless hours over the last ten years laughing, drinking wine, shopping, and having sleepovers. This day was different. Today the conversation that had taken center stage was one my mother-in-law initiated.

"What will I wear for my funeral? You know, with all these steroids my size 10/12s certainly don't fit. I am going to need something in an 18/20."

The blunt question caught us both off guard and we began to laugh nervously. My mother-in-law laughed too, even though I'm sure it took most of her strength since she was near the end of her fight. After the laugh, we realized she was serious. Always the mom on the cutting edge of fashion, she had worked at Casual Corner just so she could shop there with her paychecks. She wore the most funky and trendy accessories that most teens would have begged a month for. She was known as the foxiest dresser in our small community. Her earrings, purses, necklaces, bracelets, belts, and scarves took up an entire closet alone; she wore age appropriate, but very classy attire. It was one of the hardest things for her not being able to get dressed up and accessorize. She had tried her best, making sure she wore lipstick in a hue that matched her turbans that now covered her bald head.

On this day, it was important to her that she knew what she was wearing to her own funeral. Stunned by her desire to put together her one last party wardrobe, we laughed lightly. She adamantly told us that we needed to go out shopping. She hurried us along; we didn't know she wanted us to come back with something that evening. With even more urgency she said, "Now get going! Don't forget the accessories. You know they make the outfit!" As we walked out of her room, her last comment to us that day was, "Girls, I don't think you'll find anything in my size at Casual Corner. Why don't you try one of those nice stores that cater to the fluffy girls."

Our unplanned trip to the nearest shopping mall was sixty miles away, and as we drove, our laughter turned to tears. We talked about what colors would be best and where we should shop. When Lisa and I arrived at the mall, we hunted for something in black, as black has a way of making you look slimmer. I thought. *Isn't that funny? Still wanting to look slimmer and not even alive.* We went to the fluffy girl store where immediately a woman about the age of my mother-in-law greeted us and asked if she could be of assistance. We both looked at each other and nervously laughed again; this time we chuckled so hard we couldn't get a word out. Each time we tried to tell our clothing assistant what we wanted, we burst out in laughter. Finally, when we could hardly breathe, we blurted out at the same time, "We are looking for an outfit to wear to a funeral."

The assistant said, "Hmm, that's a tough one, I've never had that request before." After glancing at us, she added, "You know, we cater to sizes 14-24."

Lisa answered, "No, it's not for me; it is for my mother. It is for her funeral." We had completely lost our assistant. Finally when we gained back our composure, we explained the whole story and said we thought we could shop on our own.

After looking at countless dresses off the racks, and pantsuits held up to the mirror with blouses that look too old fashioned, we called it quits, thanked the assistant, and left the store. Walking by the storefront window, we noticed the mannequin on display. Simultaneously, we blurted out, "That's it! That's the outfit!"

Turning around, we went back to our assistant and asked if the outfit on the mannequin in the window came in an 18/20. Soon she came back with the selected outfit in tow. It was a beautiful black skirt with a little bounce to it accompanied by a classy black and brown leopard print cowl neck top. The look on her face was one of puzzlement and concern.

She said, "There is a small problem. The top is a body suit and snaps in the crotch."

My sister-in-law blurted out, "Mom, you're going through the pearly gates in a body suit!"

Once again, we were consumed with awkward laughter as we picked out just the right accessories, a chunky necklace and earrings. The shopping trip was topped off by the cashier, who either felt sorry for us or wanted us to get the hell out as she smiled and said, "Everything was on sale and you saved 40 percent today!" That was the deal sealer!

On the way home, we reminisced, talked about faith, our family, and how our lives would be forever changed when Lisa's mother was gone. She was leaving five children behind who would soon be orphans since my father-in-law had passed away five years earlier. We cried and in the midst of our tears, Lisa repeated, "Mom, you are going through the pearly gates in a body suit."

Arriving home, we were greeted by the nurse in the kitchen. She told us that my mother-in-law was not doing very well. We quickly grabbed our bags and headed into the room where her hospital bed was set up. Her breathing seemed to accompany that of the harp on the cassette—slow and shallow. She was laying in a position on her side, which looked uncomfortable with her head facing down looking at the floor. Lisa crawled in bed with her mother and said, "Mom, we're home. We found the perfect outfit. I think you are going to like it. Do you want to see it?"

With her eyes closed, it was all she could muster to say, "Sure." My sister-in-law began to retrieve the outfit and all of the goodies when her mother asked in a faint whisper, "Can you try it on for me?"

Closing the door, Lisa undressed as I laid out the outfit that she quietly put on, being sure to snap all four hooks on the body suit while I clasped the necklace. After Lisa was dressed and we inspected her in the mirror before giving her mother the final style show, I looked at Lisa's reflection and saw the same beauty of the woman that lay face down on the hospital bed. As the tears began to well up in Lisa, she slowly crawled down on the floor. She lay on the carpet, adjusting her bracelet, necklace, and belt. Then Lisa folded her hands over her chest in the manner that replicated someone deceased in a coffin. Through her tears in a hushed tone, she whispered to her mother, "Mom, I'm down here. I'm wearing your outfit. Look down here, Mom." Her mom barely opened her eyes. She scanned the floor trying to focus. I had crawled down to see her eyes now too. She surveyed her daughter from head to toe. Her daughter went through all the features of the outfit.

"It has a soft flowing black skirt that is not too tight and not too loose. The belt around the skirt angles down just below your waistline, Mom. Mom, do you like the top?" She lifted up the skirt and said, "Mom, look… the top is a leopard bodysuit. It's the latest thing; see, it has four snaps in the crotch? Mom, did you ever think you would go to heaven in a body suit?" Her mom smiled as much as she could muster, and fought to keep her eyes open while holding back the tears. She looked at her daughter lying on the floor and said in the faintest whisper, "Thank you, it's perfect, and I wouldn't have it any other way."

The Happy Author

Brenda Elsagher

Authors occasionally hear from readers who appreciated reading their book. They may have found it helpful from a personal standpoint or in trying to understand what a loved one might be going through.

When I wrote my first book, *If the Battle is Over, Why am I Still in Uniform?*, I knew it would be tough for my husband to let it go out in the world. It revealed a lot about our personal lives, especially some of the physical transformations I went through dealing with colorectal cancer.

It might be hard for any man to have his love life revealed, but I think he was particularly shy, coming from his Middle Eastern heritage. In Egypt, talking about body parts in mixed company was unheard of, and here I was, asking him to get comfortable with this personal information going into the public eye. Even though I am a modest person by nature, I felt it was important to write an honest telling of the physical transformational story. I didn't have anyone I knew that could relate to what I was experiencing at the time. The words colostomy, vaginal reconstruction, and hysterectomy were foreign to my vocabulary. On the edge of forty when diagnosed with cancer, my closest girlfriends and family members were just as baffled as me with the subject of the bowels. It wasn't in our daily conversation at that time. Pass the pepper; and how are your bowels today? Things have changed in that arena.

When my husband, Bahgat, and I talked about the book and how explicit it was in parts, we asked ourselves this question. Will this hurt us in any way? We figured maybe it would help others. After much discussion, we decided to go ahead and let it go out into the world as it was written. To this day, we have no regrets. It has had several reprints, and I hear from people all over the country about how much they appreciated reading it, especially the medical people. They like learning the patient's perspective on things. From this gift of writing, I get gifts every day. Not the kind that come wrapped up in a pretty bow, but a kind word, a thoughtful gesture, and sometimes a surprise comment from a nurse.

I visited my friend Debbie in the hospital. We had met thirteen years earlier in Bible study. Ironically, she, too, because of cancer, was dealing with a new ileostomy. She was about to learn how to change her pouch for the first time. The WOCN nurse came in to help teach her. Scott was a friendly guy and didn't appear too disturbed by the fact that he had an audience. Sitting in on the lesson was a nurse friend, Marilyn, and Debbie's dear friend Kathy and me.

He calmly explained the intricacies of changing the pouch properly and Debbie participated fully. She made me proud as she asked questions and calmly handled the eruptions that occurred as she learned the process. He laughed a little and told her about a book that a funny woman, from the Twin City area had written about having an ostomy. He then referred to my second book and a story about a woman who called her ostomy Vesuvius for its constant eruptions. My friends knew instantly he was talking about my books, and I just winked their silence away while I asked more questions. "What do you like about her books in particular?" I asked, feeling like a voyeur.

"She used to be a hairstylist and just the way she talks about what she is going through is so funny and honest. I recommend it to every patient I see," he said enthusiastically.

My friends couldn't stand it any longer and blurted out, "It's her—she's the one that wrote the books." He stopped what he was doing, looked right at me, and said, "When I walked into the room, I looked at you and thought you looked like the picture of the author on the back of the books and thought that would be crazy, so I didn't say anything. Wow, it's great to meet you. I really do tell every patient about your books—they're great. Brenda, they have really helped me understand the patients more."

He carried on a little while longer, and I was afraid my friend was not getting the proper attention, so we focused back on her until he was finished. It was time for me to leave and he was kind enough to walk me to the front door while we chatted on about the subject I knew nothing about fourteen years earlier. Meeting Scott that day was another precious gift I received along the way—to know that my writing makes a difference. It takes so many precious hours to write and put together a book, it's great to know the time spent was well worth it.

Thank you, dear reader, for spending your time reading these stories. I hope you found them enjoyable, enlightening, and entertaining.

Contributor Biographies

Diana Amadeo, an award winning author, sports a bit of pride in having 450 publications with her byline in books, anthologies, magazines, and newspapers. Yet, she humbly, persistently, tweaks and rewrites her thousand or so rejections with eternal hope that they may yet see the light of day. (pgs. 17-21)

Jill Amundson Winter has worked for HealthPartners for twenty-one years (half of her life!). She started in the chart room and now works as a supervisor in the Credentialing Services Bureau. It only took her six years and four college transfers to earn a B.A. in Organizational Management and Communications. (Foreword)

Jocelyn Anderson worked as an admission supervisor at Luther Hospital for twenty years. Now retired, she volunteers at the Senior Center and teaches crochet. They call themselves the Happy Hookers and she's the madam. Jocelyn is married, has four children, six grandchildren, one great grandchild, and resides in Wisconsin. E-Mail: jocey1928@live.com. (pgs. 97, 103)

Marilyn Ashenbrener, RN, has worked as a nurse for twenty-six years. Inspired by listening to friends Kathleen and Loree share their stories of nursing, Marilyn also felt a desire to help those in need. She lives in Burnsville, Minnesota, with her husband and daughter and enjoys Bible study and gardening. (pgs. 147-148)

Linda Aukett, married to Ken for twenty years, is retired from a social work career. Once editor for the *International Ostomy Association Journal*, she now volunteers for the Youth Rally Committee (helping teens with bladder and bowel disorders), the United Ostomy Associations of America (advocacy) and the Digestive Disease National Coalition. (pgs. 60-61)

David Ayres, a native of Minneapolis, is vice president of an environmental company. Surrounded in love by his wife of twenty-three years, their three teenage daughters, his sidekick Chocolate Lab and Yorkshire

Terrier, he's often found in the woods hunting, dirt biking, snowmobiling, or sailing the many lakes of Minnesota and Wisconsin. (pgs. 15-16)

Laverne H. Bardy's column, "Laverne's View," is syndicated with Senior Wire News Services, and appears monthly in *50 Plus*, a N.J. newspaper. She's written for numerous anthologies, magazines, and newspapers, and is writing a book, *Stop Telling Me I'm Old!!* She is a member of NWU, IWWG, and Women Reading Aloud. (pg. 110)

Dawn Bechtold, RN, CWOCN, is a certified wound, ostomy, continence nurse (CWOCN) since 1986. She has worked in Rapid City, Sanford, and Avera McKennan in Sioux Falls. She is the president-elect of the North Central Region (NCR) of the WOCN, and received the NCR Clinical Excellence Award in 2005. (pg. 93)

Lissa Brown spends her time observing and writing about life in the Blue Ridge Mountains of North Carolina. Writing as Leslie Brunetsky, she's the author of *Real Country, From the Fast Track to Appalachia,* a hilarious look at her transition from urban corporate warrior to rural mountain storyteller. (pgs. 27-30)

Mortimer Brown is a nine-year colorectal cancer survivor/thriver. He is active as an advocate for education, research, and legislation on behalf of fighting back. He gave testimony to the President's Commission on Cancer, works on CARRA projects, served on IRB's for his university and the NCI. Humor has always been important in his life. (pgs. 130-131)

Sheila Buska is the author of *Time Outs for Grown-ups: 5 Minute Smile-breaks*, humor columnist, and chief financial officer of Monarch School Project. Her response to a diagnosis of cancer in 2007 was to do whatever it took, as soon as possible, to get it conquered. And hey–keep those smiles coming. (pgs. 134-136)

Christina Cahall, a retired psychiatric nurse, discovered after her husband, Bill, died in 2003 her days stretched long and unfulfilled. A friend suggested she join a writing group, which has been her salvation. She keeps busy writing, participating in book club and discussion group. Christina cherishes laughter, friendships, and family. (pgs. 139-140)

Diane Cannon, has been a school teacher for twenty-eight years, has one son, Jake, age seventeen, and they live in Mesquite, Texas. She enjoys shopping for tall men, shoes, loves thrift stores and bargains. Diane is a cancer survivor since May of 2005, and feels blessed to be celebrating fifty years. (pgs. 24-25)

Shirley Cheng (b. 1983) is a blind and physically disabled award-winning author, motivational speaker, self-empowerment expert, poet, and author of eight books and contributor of fourteen. After a successful eye surgery, Shirley hopes to earn multiple science doctorates from Harvard University. Visit www.ShirleyCheng.com for more inspiration. (pgs. 156-158)

Joan Clayton is a retired elementary educator. Her ex-students have put her in Who's Who's twice. She is the author of nine books and has been published in many anthologies. She is the religion columnist for her local newspaper. Visit her website, www. joanclayton.com. (pgs. 112-113,140)

Lisa Davis spent most of her youth traveling. She works for the U.S. Department of State, roving the world. Lisa was diagnosed with colorectal cancer in 2007, resulting in an ostomy. Her faith and her husband, Jerry, gave her the strength to combat cancer and enjoy life as a person living with an ostomy. (pgs. 104-106)

Heidi Dengrove is a two-time cancer survivor whose 1999 colostomy was due to colorectal cancer. Vice president of her ostomy group for many years, she's also very active in the colorectal cancer support group she founded. Author, artist, historian-Egyptologist, horsewoman, this Jersey Girl now resides in Virginia. (pgs. 26-27)

Stephanie Devine lives in Eagan, Minnesota, with her husband, Paul, and sons Evan and Liam. She holds a BA in English from the College of St. Catherine and is presently working on a second degree in piano performance. She was diagnosed with a severe form of Crohn's disease in December 2007. (pgs. 69-70)

CONTRIBUTOR BIOGRAPHIES

Jo Diedrich, like the butterfly, Jo has been transformed through her breast cancer experience of 2000 into a writer of reflective poems. A Celtic harper who performs music for the spirit in the Twin Cities area, she has recorded a CD, *Praying Hope,* and is working on a second. Contact her at jadbutter@aol.com (pgs. 160-161)

Regis DiGiacomo is a retired electrical engineer of General Electric Healthcare and Marquette Medical Systems where he designed patient monitoring equipment for hospital intensive care units for over thirty years. He is currently doing research studies at Marquette University. He is married and has two sons and six grandchildren. (pg 104)

Dennis Douda is an Emmy-winning TV news anchor and reporter. Since 1999 he has headed up the Health Care/Medical reporting unit at CBS-owned station WCCO-TV in Minneapolis. (pgs.63-65)

Jude Ebbinghaus has an ileostomy due to ulcerative colitis and rheumatoid arthritis. She manages it successfully with aqua therapy, meds, and a positive attitude. A literacy specialist, she has been married to Charlie for thirty years, has two daughters, Alycia and Cheryl, and loves to volunteer! (pgs. 97-99)

Bahgat Elsagher, originally from Egypt, has lived in the USA since 1983 and works in the computer field. Married to the author for twenty years, he is a master of puns, and enjoys a good laugh—especially at his own jokes. Bahgat is father to their children, John and Jehan. (pgs. 85-86)

Eugene Elsen (Hump) has been married to Helen for nearly fifty-four years. They have eight children and ten grandchildren. Hump worked with his brothers at a service station for twenty-nine years before becoming a financial planner. Retired, he enjoys playing cards with Helen, doing the crypto quips, and visiting with family and friends. (pgs. 76-78)

Judy Epstein is an award-winning humor columnist who lives on Long Island, New York, with her husband and two children. Luckily for her, medical troubles stimulate her funny bone–and her pen. All's well that ends up as grist for the mill. Catch more of her adventures at www.alookonthelightside.com. (pgs. 52-56, 110-112, 118-119)

Jon Eveslage lives in Burnsville, Minnesota, with wife, Pat; son, Paul; and daughter, Elena. He was born and raised in west central Minnesota in Frazee, where he still enjoys summer weekends at the family lake cabin. Jon works as a project lead for Thomson-Reuters in Eagan, Minnesota. (pgs. 49-50)

Lois Fink is a motivational speaker who shares her moving story about her nineteen-year battle with Crohn's disease. Ostomy surgery, at thirty-six, gave her back everything Crohn's disease had taken away—a full, rewarding life. Fink shares inspirations she learned along the uneven path to better health with her audiences. (pgs. 14-15)

Kathy Fritz graduated from nursing school at the age of forty-five and presently works for Fairview Ridges Clinic in Burnsville, Minnesota. She has been married to a great guy, Bud, for thirty-four years. They love to travel and reside in Eagan, Minnesota, with their dog, Annie. (pgs. 13-14, 138)

Annette Geroy, after thirty-two years as a teacher in public education, now works extensively with women who have suffered sexual abuse as a lay minister with Mount Horeb House Ministries in Kerrville, TX. Her recently published book, *Looking With New Eyes*, examines her personal healing journey from childhood sexual abuse. (pgs. 44-46)

Pamela Goldstein had a twenty-year nursing career then turned to her passion—writing. Pam has several short stories accepted for publications—two are in *Chicken Soup for Empty Nesters*. Her radio show, "Boker Tov," from Windsor/Detroit, is heard worldwide via Internet. E-mail Pam at boker_tov2002@yahoo.ca. (pgs. 58-60, 148-150)

Pamela Gregg is communication administrator for the University of Dayton Research Institute (world's best place to work) and proud mother of opera singer Bree Sprankle. A former feature writer and columnist for the *Dayton Daily News*, she now enjoys the challenge of learning about, then publicizing, advances in science. Laughter helps. (pgs. 71-72)

Carol Gustke holds a Bachelor of Science degree in human services from Western Michigan University. Her slice-of-life stories have appeared in

Woman's World and *Christian Singles*. Her contribution to this anthology is taken from Helium, an online writing site. Her new book, *An Angel's First Job*, can be viewed at www.carolgustkebooks.com (pgs. 116-117)

Cappy Hall Rearick is a humor columnist, and has authored six columns: "Alive And Well In Hollywood," "Tidings," "Simply Southern," "Simply Senior," "Putin' On The Gritz," and "Simply Something," a monthly e-column. She has three books in print: *Simply Southern, Simply Southern Ease,* and *Simply Christmas.* Cappy lives in St. Simons Island, Georgia. (pgs. 6-9)

K. Ann Hambridge was born, educated, and worked in Scotland until immigration as a widowed, middle-aged grandmother moved to Calgary in December 1994 on her marriage to Mark. A three-time colon cancer survivor, Ann walks her deep Christian faith in supporting ostomates and others in crisis and helping immigrants to integrate. (pgs. 99-102)

Claribel Hawkins was born March 18, 1923, and married Martin Hawkins on December 25, 1941. Together they had two daughters and she is now blessed with five grandchildren and eight great-grandchildren. Martin died in 2002, and Claribel continues to live on the farm in the Mississippi delta. She is a member of Isola Baptist Church. (pgs. 92-93)

Sterling Haynes, M.D. graduated in medicine fifty years ago, practiced in British Columbia and Alabama, and started writing at age seventy. He writes a humorous column for the newspaper and his poetry and stories have won awards. Haynes has been published by *Caitlin Press,* the *Harvard Medical Alumni Journal,* The *Medical Post, Okanagan Life, Family Practice,* and *Alberta Views.* (pgs. 66-67)

Joanne Heitzman was a recently retired grandma when diagnosed with a rare cancer, leiomyosarcoma. Intent on enjoying her four grandchildren, she made up her mind to not let a colostomy or urinary diversion get the best of her, even learning how to balance one grandchild on each knee for story time. (pgs. 99)

Craig Hergert teaches writing and popular culture at Minneapolis Community and Technical College and is known for using humor in his courses. He has performed standup comedy professionally, has staged productions of his own comedy sketches three times in the Twin Cities, and has written for Garrison Keillor's. *A Prairie Home Companion.* (pgs. 126-129)

Vince Hopkins is a regional development director for Xavier University in Cincinnati, Ohio. He lives with his wife Julie, and three children, Judd, Aaron, and Abbey, in Mason, Ohio. His mother-in-law, Vivian Riestenberg, continues to inspire her entire family. (pgs. 131-134)

Karen Hopkinson, RN, BSN, has been a nurse since 1984. She works for Hollister Incorporated and part-time at Advocate Good Shepherd Hospital. Married to John for twenty-five years, they are blessed with two beautiful children. Karen enjoys running, golf, tennis, and spending time with her family and friends. (pgs. 93-97)

Janie Jasin, CSP, is a speaker, consultant, and author of the best seller, *The Littlest Christmas Tree.* Jasin has delivered wise words and laughter for over thirty years. Audiences of teens, families, seniors, health care professionals, corporate moguls, and associations have reveled in her wit and wisdom. www.janiespeaks.com. (pgs. 88-89)

Ellen Javernick is a second grade teacher in Loveland, Colorado, and the author of more than twenty books for children. Ellen's newest book, *The Birthday Pet,* was written while she was the Granny Nanny for Matt's little girl while he was at Walter Reed. (pgs. 61-62)

Cheryl Jobe is a granddaughter and great-granddaughter of pioneers, Indians, Confederates, and immigrants. Strong in faith and will, soft in heart. Cheryl married her high school sweetheart out of spite because he wouldn't go steady. A burr under his saddle ever since. Mid-fifties, graying, and dumpy, but ain't life grand! (pgs. 40-42)

LaDonna Joseph enjoyed the medical profession for thirty-five years. During that time she went on a medical mission to Lima, Peru, to help children with cleft lips and palates. She likes to cook and travel, and has a daughter who lives nearby in Inver Grove Heights, Minnesota. (pg. 79)

CONTRIBUTOR BIOGRAPHIES

Mark Kennedy from Chicago began his lifelong study of the Japanese language and culture at Bates College. He studied in Japan as a Fulbrighter and married his wife, Naomi, a former nurse, after meeting her on a sales call for Hollister Incorporated where he has worked for more than sixteen years. (pg. 73)

Brenda Kuhlman credits her dad with nurturing her unique sense of humor, a skill that helped her through ostomy surgery for Crohn's disease at age twenty. Thirty-two years later, her one regret? Not purchasing stock in ostomy supplies back then. Brenda is a part-time writer and educator, living in Northern Virginia with her husband, Jack. (pg. 78)

David Lang, M.D. is a family practiner who has been serving patients for twenty-five years. He continues to enjoy exercise and has a deeper appreciation for the love of his family and caregivers in general. He resides in Lakeville, Minnesota, with his wife, has six grown daughters, and is a happy grandfather. (pgs. 34-36)

Carol Larson, cancer survivor, has written three books: *When the Trip Changes, Positive Options for Colorectal Cancer,* and *Life Lines—Keeping Your Head above Water.* In 2008, Carol received the Breaking Boundaries Award from the Colorectal Cancer Coalition and is currently president of the Ostomy Association of the Minneapolis Area (OAMA). (pgs. 22-23)

Lori La Bey is a national speaker and owns Senior Lifestyle Trends, a Minnesota-based company. Her goal is to reduce combative behaviors by identifying stress triggers to create remarkable moments for seniors. She uses humor to show audiences how to implement key tips and techniques through personal stories. www.SeniorLifestyleTrends.com (pgs. 153-154, 158-160, 162-163)

Sari Legge lives in Rhode Island with husband, Peter Legge, and their son, Jacob. Legge is a retired broadcast announcer with visions of a comeback! She writes "Sari Says," advice column for CCFA's Take Charge magazine, founded "Dear Baggy" on IBDSucks.org, and is treasurer for IBD Quilt Project, Inc. (pgs. 87-88, 119-121)

Richard Lewis is the president and founder of Church Treasurers of Canada, Inc. and as a speaker, consultant, and author, he addresses the financial accounting problems of churches and charities. Email: rlewis@ churchtreasurers.ca. Web: www.churchtreasurers.ca (pgs. 146-147)

Carol Malzahn is a forty-six-year-old mother and wife. She survived Crohn's colitis for twelve years before having surgery in 2005. She currently splits her time between substitute teaching, volunteering with the Crohn's & Colitis Foundation of America, and being treasurer for the Home Owner's Association and the women's board at church. (pgs. 23-24)

Michael Mangano is a former advertising copywriter/creative director, who has won every major creative award, as well as having work represented in the Smithsonian Institute's permanent collection. He taught creative advertising at New York's School of Visual Arts. A short story of his was published in the *Crocodile Review*. (pgs. 25-26)

Jaimie Mattes was diagnosed with colon cancer at age thirty-two in 2002. Designated Mr. May 2009, of the Colondar, (a calendar for survivors under fifty), he is married with two children. Active in Get Your Rear in Gear, The Colon Club, and the American Cancer Society, Jamie's an advocate of exercise to stay healthy. (pg. 163)

Kay Mickel lives in California near Yosemite National Park. Diagnosed with ovarian cancer stage 3C in August of 2006, she's written a series of stories about her cancer journey for her local newspaper and now passionately shares her faith and cancer story to churches in her area. And she laughs! (pgs. 129-130)

Avamarie Miller is a mother, wife, animal lover, registered nurse, and humor writer who lives in Texas. She loves every minute of her life, and has finally accepted her birthday suit will never fit like it did when she was nineteen years old. Visit avamariemiller@yahoo.com. (pgs. 50-51)

Eileen Mitchell is a 2008 Robert Benchley Society Award finalist, 2006 Will Rogers finalist, and winner of the 2007 Thurber humor writing contest. Author of *The Amazing, Incredible, Shrinking, Colossal, Bikini-*

CONTRIBUTOR BIOGRAPHIES

Crazed CREATURE FROM THE PUBLIC DOMAIN, also writes the FILM HOUND blog for the *Seattle Post-Intelligencer* online. Visit: emitchellhumor.com (pgs. 67-68)

Carol McAdoo Rehme never bandaged her dolls; she urged her children to save their accidents for their dad's attention. Now a grandma, she's relieved to pass the torch of responsibility to the next generation. A veteran editor and author, Carol's latest book is *Chicken Soup for the Empty Nester's Soul* (2008). www.rehme.com (pgs. 42-43, 68-69, 121-123)

Barbara Jay Nies was published in the *Detroit News* Young Writers Club when she was eight. At fifty-nine, she published *Finding Ways: Recovering From Rheumatoid Arthritis Through Alternative Medicine.* In 2009, at seventy-one, Nies' memoir called *Wild Strawberries and Poison Ivy: Coming Up Common in Warren Township* will be published. (pgs. 82-83)

Linda O'Connell has a positive attitude and sense of humor. She is a wife, mother, grandmother, and seasoned early childhood educator in St. Louis, Missouri. Linda refers to her wrinkles as laugh lines from her students and family. Her work appears in numerous inspirational anthologies, mainstream and literary magazines, and books. billin7@juno.com (pgs. 113-115)

Jill Olson grew up in Burley, Idaho. She is a twenty-two-year-old senior at Idaho State University studying dietetics. She loves nutrition and is the vice president of their Dietetics Club on campus. She loves to read and play the piano. (pgs.102-103)

Bob and Vella Owens have been married fifty-five years, and they live part-time in Arizona. Originally from Colorado, they raised six children and twenty-one foster children. They enjoy swimming, walking, hiking, and are active in their neighborhood and church. They enjoy life and praise God for his blessings. (pg. 10)

Jay Pacitti is a former lawyer who now works to empower people with Crohn's, colitis, and ostomies. Since this story event, Jay has transitioned to male. He appreciates his good health and credits his positive attitude, sense of humor, and straightforward communication with doctors for remaining (mostly) in remission. (pgs.106-108)

Suzanne Pawlak is a sometime writer and full-time surgical tech in Columbus, Ohio, where she lives with her husband of thirty years and four cats. She has had many careers, but this story happened during her very first job after graduating from Ohio State. (pg. 58)

Mia Probst graduated as a certified radiologic technologist in 1971. After working for a few years, she left to become a homemaker. Mia returned to the workforce in 1990, and became certified as a mammographer and has enjoyed serving the women in her community by providing quality mammography imaging. (pgs. 51-52)

Paris Purnell currently works as a marketing manager for Global Consumer Care Programs at Hollister Incorporated, in Illinois, USA. Originally from Australia, Paris commenced his career in nursing and specialized in colorectal surgical nursing, gaining certification in stomal therapy (WOCN). He currently resides in Evanston, Illinois, with his pet fish. (pgs. 37, 44, 71, 78-79)

Debby Reisinger lives in Apple Valley, Minnesota. She works in customer relations and puts her creative writing skills to use responding to customer complaints. She has recently become an Irish citizen, has two granddogs, and is *patiently* waiting for one of her children to make her and her husband grandparents. (pgs. 30-31)

Joyce Richardson received her MA in creative writing from Ohio University. She is the author of an Appalachian novel, *On Sunday Creek,* and a tarot chapbook, *The Reader.* She enjoys painting, traveling, and hanging out with her writer-husband, Phil. Joyce is the wife and mother of clowns. (pgs. 10-13)

Steve Roberts spent three decades in the U.S auto industry, followed by ten years as a business consultant. Lately he has been writing two memoirs, two action adventure novels, and has numerous short stories, and articles to his credit. Roberts works for several non-profits and is president of the Dearborn Library Foundation. www.steverroberts.com (pg. 21)

Renee Rongen is an award winning humorist, inspirational speaker, author, and radio talk show host. She has been featured in numerous national publications and is the international spokesperson for the Pay it Forward Foundation. She is Mom to three and wife to one and lives on a peaceful lake in northern Minnesota. www.reneerongen.com (pgs. 154-155, 164-167)

Dorothy Rosby is an entertaining speaker and syndicated humor columnist whose work appears regularly in newspapers in eleven western and midwestern states. She lives in Rapid City, South Dakota, with her husband and son. (pgs. 83-85, 86-87)

Darlene Roy-Johnson is a professional trainer and life coach, empowering women to succeed in ways they never dreamed of. She resides in Apple Valley, Minnesota.(pg. 62)

Alanna Seppelt of Inver Grove Heights, Minnesota, has been a registered nurse for eight years and a CWOCN for three. Currently, Alanna is completing her master's degree in nursing to become an adult/geriatric nurse practitioner. In her spare time, she likes to travel, kickbox, and volunteer. (pg. 51)

Bob Simpson writes the weekly Arkansas newspaper column "Hogspore Community News," the National Society of Newspaper Columnists first place humor column for 2008. Bob, Trisha, and daughters, Catlin and Hannah, live in Largo, Florida, on McKay Creek. We eat chocolate cake all day and fish all night. Visit www.hogspore.com. (pgs. 16-17)

Shirley Stille, RN, CWOCN, CFCN from Aitkin, Minnesota, has been in nursing for thirty-five years. She has worked in acute, long-term care, public health, and home care and achieved her dream of getting her CWOCN in 2005. She dedicates these stories to her many patients and co-workers. (pgs. 63, 138-139,145)

Hope Sunderland is a registered nurse whose specialty was critical care. She recently retired her bedpan and enema bucket and hung up her scrubs. A freelance writer, she lives in South Texas where she writes what she hopes is humor. (pgs. 141-144)

Rox Tarrant is a rehabilitation consultant in Minneapolis, Minnesota, by day and is a talented comedian and producer by night. Rox is well known for providing opportunities for rising female comics as well as veterans in her highly acclaimed performances of *Women Out All Night*. www.roxtarrant.com (pgs. 37-40)

Ginger Truitt is a humor columnist and speaker residing in central Indiana. Her column appears weekly in several newspapers and won a 2006 award from the Hoosier State Press Association for Best General Column. For more stories from Ginger, visit www.gingertruitt.com. (pgs. 115-116)

Carole Turner is a reviewer for *The Book Report Network* and a freelance writer whose articles have appeared in *Kelleys Life, Lifestyles 2000, Green-Prints*, and *Country Living*. She lives with her husband and a very spoiled cat on Kelleys Island, Ohio, in Lake Erie. (pgs. 47-48)

Dan Tyrrell is a seventy-four-year-old retired automotive engineer. Was born, raised, and received a BME degree (GM Institute), in Michigan. He currently resides in Salem Township, a rural suburb of the automotive capital. During 2008, Dan was hospitalized at the Cleveland Clinic for abdominal surgery. (pg.144)

Midge Willson, RN, MSN, is a midwestern CWOCN with over two decades of acute care hospital experience directly caring for those who have new ostomies as well as those who may develop ostomy management issues. Midge is employed as a manager of clinical education for Hollister Incorporated. (pgs. 146)

About the Author

Brenda Elsagher is the author of *If the Battle is Over, Why am I Still in Uniform?* Now in its fourth printing, this book first came out in 2003. It is a funny and poignant memoir of Brenda's experience of learning she had colorectal cancer at age thirty-nine. She takes the reader on her journey with her as she adjusts to the many physical and emotional changes along the way.

Brenda's second book, *I'd like to Buy a Bowel Please!*, now in its second printing, was first released in April of 2006. This anthology is a collection of over eighty stories of hope and humor in dealing with life-altering operations resulting in ostomy surgery. Each contributor's challenge was to write about something funny that happened while living with an ostomy.

Brenda is a professional writer and international keynote speaker. With comedy as her background, her presentations are filled with belly laughs and thoughtful stories. If you would like her to present at your next conference, contact her through the information below.

Brenda Elsagher: www.livingandlaughing.com
Brenda@livingandlaughing.com. Office: 952-882-9882